Law and Society
Recent Scholarship

Edited by Melvin I. Urofsky

A Series from LFB Scholarly

Video Surveillance: Power and Privacy in Everyday Life

Bilge Yesil

LFB Scholarly Publishing LLC
El Paso 2009

Library of Congress Cataloging-in-Publication Data

Yesil, Bilge, 1973-
Video surveillance : power and privacy in everyday life / Bilge Yesil.
p. cm. -- (Law & society)
Includes bibliographical references and index.
ISBN 978-1-59332-370-7 (hardcover : alk. paper)
1. Video surveillance--United States. I. Title.

TK6680.3.Y47 2009
363.2'32--dc22
2009032646

ISBN 978-1-59332-370-7

Printed on acid-free 250-year-life paper.

Manufactured in the United States of America.

TABLE OF CONTENTS

ACKNOWLEDGEMENTS

This book owes its existence to many individuals. Ted Magder, Helen Nissenbaum, and Colleen Larson provided unparalleled support, careful reading and incisive questioning. I am grateful for their shaping role in this project. I also wish to thank Allen Feldman, Nicholas Mirzoeff, Arvind Rajagopal for generously sharing their time and intellect with me, and Mark Crispin Miller and Aurora Wallace for offering insights into this project at its early stages.

Research for this book was undertaken while I was the recipient of a National Science Foundation grant, and I wish to thank the National Science Foundation—Societal Dimensions for Engineering, Science, and Technology Program for its support.

Conversations I had with Mark Andrejevic, Rodney Benson, Joellen Fisherkeller, Kelly Gates, James Hay, Anna McCarthy, Charlton McIlwain, Sue Murray, Ayse Oncu, Siva Vaidhyanathan and Caitlin Zaloom helped me in innumerable ways. Terry Moran helped me arrange interviews with New York City Police Department officers. I gratefully acknowledge his assistance.

I also thank Allison Butler, Cheryl Casey, Sue Collins, Christina Kotchemidova, Bill Phillips, MJ Robinson, Eric Saranovitz and Marion Wrenn for their support, and Sam Howard-Spink, David Parisi and Michael Zimmer for their feedback.

I put the finishing touches to this book at the Department of Media Culture, College of Staten Island—City University of New York, where my colleagues provided a collegial and supportive environment.

I am also grateful to Bahar Eris, Karin Karakasli, Sevim Yesil, Hakki Yesil for always championing my efforts, and Mustafa Yesil for keeping me up to date with surveillance stories from around the world. But I owe my most substantive thanks to Victor Duong for his unconditional support.

Last but not least, I wish to express my gratitude to my research participants. I cannot thank them by name, but I am grateful to each and every school administrator, student, police officer, park visitor who took the time to talk to me and in the meantime taught me so much about surveillance, privacy and power.

CHAPTER 1

Introduction

In September 2002, millions of people watched Madelyn Toogood, a 25-year-old mother, slap and punch her four-year-old daughter Martha in the back seat of her SUV. Martha's beating was captured by surveillance cameras in the parking lot of a Kohl's department store in Indiana, which recorded every shocking detail. The surveillance tape was made public by the police in order to find the mother and daughter, and was played on local and national news programs repeatedly for eight days. In the end, Toogood turned herself in after seven days in the public eye.[1]

The release of the tape by the police and the media's looping of the surveillance imagery ad nauseam helped to flush out a potentially violent mother, but it also did more than that. In a subtler way, the crime control establishment made up of law enforcement and private security businesses (and in other instances, community groups such as neighborhood watch), in concert with local and national media eager for good visuals, achieved another, more important objective. They reminded potential wrongdoers and the general populace that they too were under surveillance—anytime, anywhere. Before she started beating her daughter, Toogood was seen on tape looking around to make sure no one could see her. This most condemning detail invited audiences to embrace the power of surveillance, and to watch their behaviors when in public. The lesson was clear: there is always someone watching even if you cannot see them.

From the 1970s onwards, and especially over the past ten years, the use of video surveillance cameras in numerous settings and by various entities—government and non-government alike—has become widespread in certain public settings such as streets, parks, plazas, housing projects, schools and public transportation areas. Law enforcement agencies and private actors use video surveillance to reduce and/or prevent crime and to gather evidence and manage the deployment of police and other security personnel. After the events of

September 11, 2001, law enforcement at federal and local levels turned to video surveillance (and face recognition software) as part of their general security measures to prevent terrorist acts.[2] Private entities, such as retail stores, malls, banks, hospitals, hotels and businesses that want to protect their property use video surveillance to deter theft and vandalism, monitor employees for productivity, and/or protect the company from liability. Some nursing homes and daycare centers use video surveillance to monitor staff and to reassure the public that their loved ones are receiving quality care. In addition to these institutionalized practices of video surveillance, which take place in public settings, there are private individuals and groups who use surveillance cameras. These include parents who use nanny cams in their own homes to monitor childcare providers, and neighborhood watch groups or gated communities that deploy cameras to keep criminals away from their neighborhood and/or catch them in the act.

Despite its ubiquity, video surveillance is not without its critics. Criminologists themselves are far from unanimous on the effects of video surveillance. Surveys in Britain and in the United States have found that following the installation of surveillance cameras, criminals—actual and potential—leave that area (NACRO 2002, ACLU 2008, CITRIS 2008). It may be that video surveillance doesn't so much reduce crime as displace it. In a similar vein, independent evaluations have found that camera systems have little or no impact on prevention or reduction of violent crimes (NACRO 2002, Rice-Oxley 2004). Privacy advocates and civil liberties groups argue that surveillance cameras pose serious threats to privacy and individual freedoms. They direct attention to how operators might abuse video surveillance systems by focusing unduly on ethnic minorities or by leering at women; how surveillance imagery might fall into the wrong hands, and how law enforcement might start using the system in covert ways to gather information about political dissidents or social outsiders. Critics contend that the expanding use of video surveillance might eventually lead to greater erosion of civil liberties and strip individuals of any expectation of privacy in public places.[3] Further, they direct attention to function creep, a term used to explain how surveillance cameras installed for one purpose might eventually be used for other purposes. For example, cameras initially deployed by a company to prevent trespassing can later on be used to monitor the movements of employees.

Despite the concerns regarding efficacy, civil liberties and privacy, video surveillance is nevertheless welcomed, supported or at least largely accepted by public opinion. Its champions, both public authorities and private actors, render it as a safety tool that they need to use to prevent crime, protect assets, ensure safety, etc. They construct video surveillance as a quick technological fix to the problem of crime, and assert that privacy concerns are simply the price of security, and should not be privileged over the greater good.

In the 1960s and '70s, surveillance was generally seen in a negative light—a manifestation of government intrusion into the daily lives of individuals. This unease had flourished in a social and political environment shaped by Cold War anxieties, political witch-hunts, and a general sense of suspicion. It had also been prompted by such developments as the FBI's extensive wiretapping of political dissidents and collection of personal information about thousands of ordinary individuals, as well as the Watergate scandal that resulted from Richard Nixon's operatives' use of electronic "bugs" to listen in on Democratic officials (*Someone's Watching*, 2004).

Negative attitudes were also amplified by the fact that the benefits of surveillance had yet to come into full view. For example, neither information systems nor their benefits (the convenience of credit cards, for example) were especially widespread, making it difficult to tout the positive aspects of surveillance. However, as electronic/data monitoring techniques began to penetrate every aspect of modern life in the early 1980s, surveillance came to be seen in a different light: it was not about government intrusion, but about making life easier and more convenient (Rule 2007). The erstwhile general discomfort with surveillance in the 1970s gave way to acceptance in the 1980s and '90s, mostly through the argument that surveillance works in the public interest by providing benefits such as convenience, access to services and safety.

It can be argued that video surveillance benefited from this general acquiescence to electronic/data surveillance in the 1980s and 90s. Given the political climate of suspicion in the 1970s, the images conjured by video surveillance – a relatively new technology by then – were mostly of Big Brother and totalitarianism. According to a 1978 Gallup poll, only 10% of the population felt comfortable with video surveillance. Over the next two decades, video surveillance came to be regarded more approvingly. By 1997, 52% of those polled by Gallup said they supported video surveillance in public places (Ward 1998). More recently, and especially after the terrorist attacks of September 11, public approval of video surveillance as a security measure has been at an all-time high. A Zogby poll in March 2002 found that 79% of the respondents favored the use of video surveillance of public places to combat terrorism (Zogby International 2002). According to a CBS News poll conducted in April 2002, 77% of the respondents said they would approve of government agencies or police departments installing video cameras in public places to prevent terrorist attacks. A further 49% said cameras would help reduce crime in general (CBS News 2002). A 2006 Zogby International poll found that 80% of respondents would permit video surveillance of public places (Zogby International 2006). According to a 2007 Washington Post/ ABC News poll, 71% of respondents support having public surveillance cameras while 25% do not (Washington Post/ABC News 2007).

Given the growing prevalence of video surveillance systems in public spaces, the complex social phenomena they produce, and the public support they garner, more systematic academic research in the United States context is warranted.

Leading scholars who address surveillance technologies, their applications and social outcomes in the U.S. context focus mostly on computers, databases and networks, and Internet and e-mail monitoring.[4] In comparison to this sustained literature on electronic/data surveillance, video surveillance has generally been explored as one of the dimensions of the larger surveillance apparatus.[5] For example, Marx (1990) discusses video surveillance within the framework of undercover police surveillance, while Staples (1997), Whitaker (1999) and Parenti (2003) explore it as one of the many components of surveillance society alongside with Internet and e-mail monitoring, and collection of personal data. Jensen and Draffan (2004), Zureik and Salter (2006), Webb (2007), Lyon (2007), and O'Hara and Shadbolt (2008) make references to video surveillance while investigating the post-September 11 computer surveillance, data mining and privacy issues. In a similar vein, edited volumes by Haggerty and Ericson (2006), Monahan (2006), Hier and Greenberg (2007), and Aas, Oppen and Lomell (2008) discuss video surveillance as part of a larger framework of contemporary surveillance focusing on theoretical debates in surveillance studies, proliferation of various forms of surveillance in different spheres of life, and social changes brought about by surveillance. Deviating from this general body of work on surveillance, control and privacy, McGrath (2004) investigates video surveillance from the perspective of art, performance and social space, aiming to understand the pleasures of surveillance in popular culture, while Andrejevic (2007) discusses surveillance and web cameras within the context of digitization and interactive media.

Outside the academic literature, exclusive studies of video surveillance have been conducted by civil liberties, privacy advocacy and activist groups, and university research centers. The Electronic Privacy Information Center and the American Civil Liberties Union prepare and publish reports on the intensification of video surveillance in public spaces, and organize lectures or conferences with the aim of raising questions about the effectiveness of this technology and its consequences on civic life.[6]

Activists and performance artists are also engaged in criticism of video surveillance. For example, the Surveillance Camera Players of New York City, an activist group formed in 1996, protests against video surveillance through brief performances delivered in front of surveillance cameras on subway stations or public streets. The group also offers "Surveillance Camera Outdoor Walking Tours" of heavily monitored neighborhoods in Manhattan as a way of informing the public of the use and outcomes of surveillance cameras. Such activist/artistic praxis has inspired others in the United States (San Francisco, Tempe) and the world (Stockholm, Bologna) to form their own groups to protest against cameras or offer walking tours.[7]

More recently, the Institute for Applied Autonomy, a group of engineers and artists, has been offering projects and products for activists. Among these projects, iSee should be of particular interest to surveillance activists. It is a web-based application that looks up "paths of least surveillance" in cities like Manhattan and London, so citizens can walk around the city without fear of being "caught on tape."[8]

The considerable increase in the use of video surveillance in the post-September 11 era has also motivated university research centers to conduct independent studies on surveillance and crime related issues. In 2008, the University of Southern California School of Policy, Planning and Development released a report on the effects of video surveillance on crime in two areas of Los Angeles. The study examined about a dozen cameras and found no significant impact on crime.[9] In 2008, the Center for Information Technology Research in the Interest of Society (CITRIS) and the Samuelson Clinic at the University of California, Berkeley conducted an independent study of San Francisco's small surveillance system of 68 cameras. According to this study, cameras appear to have had a small impact on property crimes, but no impact on violent crimes (CITRIS, 2008).

In light of the literature I have briefly described above, systematic studies on video surveillance in the U.S. context are definitely warranted. This book aims to contribute to video surveillance literature by analyzing socio-political dimensions of the development and deployment of video surveillance, and by exploring socio-cultural questions concerning privacy, autonomy and agency. Most importantly, this study aims to make an intervention in the public debate on video surveillance and privacy, which has centered primarily on benefits of surveillance but not on citizens' everyday experiences of power, control and privacy. Public and private entities who use cameras argue that video surveillance makes public spaces safer, and highlight the promise of surveillance. On the other hand, privacy advocates and civil libertarians argue that video surveillance in public spaces constitutes a breach of the right to privacy. Surveillance cameras in public spaces are almost always discussed in terms of either security needs or legal protection of privacy, but not contextualized within larger social, political or cultural dynamics. In this study. rather than reiterating the technical, legal discourse on surveillance and privacy issues, I offer a critical analysis bringing to the foreground the voices of people who are engaged in the politics of video surveillance and of those who experience its effects in everyday life.

"Eye in the Sky"

Surveillance is the systematic investigation or monitoring of the actions or communications of one or more persons. Its primary objective is to collect information about the individuals concerned, their activities or actions. Its secondary purpose is to deter a whole population from engaging in certain kinds of activities (Clarke 1997, Lyon 1994, Lyon 2007). Surveillance can be undertaken by public or private entities, in different domains that range from administration, commerce, and employment to policing and security (Lyon 1994, Monahan 2006, Lyon 2007).

Video surveillance, on the other hand, refers to the continuous, systematic and remote monitoring of people and spaces through the use of video technology.[10] Typically, video surveillance consists of a video camera with zoom lenses; a recording device such as a videocassette recorder (VCR); and a monitor that displays these recorded images for real-time or subsequent viewing. Additional features can also enhance the capabilities of any given video surveillance system. Among these are next generation cameras with improved pan, tilt and zoom lenses; computer programs that allow captured and recorded images to be viewed at a distant or central location; software that enables digital images to be transmitted over the Internet; night-vision technology that captures images in the dark at daylight levels of clarity; bullet-proof casings and automated self-defense mechanisms that protect surveillance equipment; motion detectors that place the system on high alert when anything moves in view of the cameras; and digitized recording systems that match video camera signals with images in databases. In recent years, there has been a proliferation of "smart" CCTV (Closed Circuit Television), which is basically video surveillance coupled with face recognition software. In this system, cameras capture facial images and send a video signal to the software, which then compares those images against a database of facial images of criminals, terrorists, wanted persons, etc. In cases of an algorithmic match above a certain level of confidence, the system sounds an alarm signaling to the system operator that there is a match.[11]

The precedent to video surveillance is visual surveillance by the human eye conducted without the use of cameras and recording devices, such as a police officer monitoring a given space and the people in it only with his eyes. When we are subject to visual surveillance by the human eye, in most cases we have knowledge of the direct observer who is working in the service of a given institution, entity or actor. For example, when we see a uniformed police officer patrolling a public park we know where s/he is, what s/he is looking at, and whether or not s/he is looking at us. But when we are subject to video surveillance, the direct observer is typically invisible and unverifiable to us. We do not know who it is, where s/he is located, whether or not s/he is looking at us. In video surveillance systems, the observer is not embodied or subjectivized, but replaced by a camera. Further, video surveillance is distinct from surveillance by the human eye because cameras and recording devices make surveillance more extensive, more efficient and less obtrusive by overcoming the limits of space and time.

Video surveillance is used in different ways, and for different purposes, which I refer to as *indiscriminate* and *discriminate*. Indiscriminate video surveillance, which is the subject matter of this book, seeks to monitor a place in general and all the persons and their activities, behaviors, and movements within it. Public authorities and private entities use indiscriminate surveillance in public streets, parks, worksites, retail environments, schools, airports, etc., covertly or overtly, to ensure safety and security, protect property and eliminate undesired behaviors and generate desired ones. Here surveillance cameras are typically in plain sight and deployed permanently, sometimes accompanied by signs that say, "These premises are under camera surveillance."

Discriminate video surveillance aims to track a particular person or a group of persons by using surveillance cameras covertly. For example, the police deploy plain clothes officers with hidden or visible cameras, mount hidden cameras on utility poles, plant them in private quarters or station non-descript vehicles equipped with them in a particular location to record the position and actions of persons of interest. Private detectives also engage in similar practices—to the extent allowed by the law—and monitor and record the activities and actions of a particular person. Here the objective is to collect information about the person in question and to use the video footage for evidentiary purposes. Typically, in these cases video surveillance is used on a need basis, that is, temporarily and for the duration of tracking.

In the following pages, I also discuss the *watchers* and the *watched*. By *watchers*, I refer to those who use video surveillance or are responsible for its deployment, use, operation, etc. This includes government agencies, law enforcement officials and state and local police departments; employers and management in private corporations, airports, malls, stores, nursing homes and daycare centers; school superintendents and administrators; small-business owners; parents, gated communities, neighborhood watch groups, business improvement districts and community groups who are fully or in part engaged in the ownership, deployment and operation of video surveillance cameras.

The *watched,* on the other hand, refers to individuals or groups who are the target of video surveillance in a given public setting. They are employees, students, nursing home staff, babysitters, sales clerks, shoppers, drivers, park-goers, etc., who are monitored, either selectively or arbitrarily.

The Panopticon and Beyond

Scholarly literature generally relies on Michel Foucault's theoretical model of the Panopticon to understand the driving forces behind, and the implications of video surveillance. This model is inspired by Jeremy Bentham's prison design that dates back to the 18th century. Bentham, a British philosopher, was particularly concerned with the demobilization of populations and associated crime waves of the 18th century. In *An Introduction to the Principles of Morals and Legislation* (1781), he directed attention to the inadequacy of coerced compliance or corporal punishment, and called for a new form of punishment that was not to cause pain or suffering, but to set an example and bring about reform. Bentham recognized that in order to deter others by force of example, punishment had to be made as rational as possible so that it would be supported by the public (Bentham 1781, 412). Punishment should no longer be an act of wrath or vengeance, but of calculation and discipline.

This idea of rational punishment was also the core concept of *The Panopticon Writings,* in which Bentham described his plans for the Panopticon—a prison run like a factory, as a capitalist enterprise. The Panopticon was a rotunda-form circular building with cells on the circumference. Its center went all the way up to the inspection tower where the inspector was concealed from observation of prisoners by blinds, but could survey the whole building. To deter prisoners from transgressing, the Panopticon relied on the "apparent omnipresence of the inspector" but not his real presence. This was how the Panopticon differed from ordinary prisons: the inspector's power derived from his invisibility. The important element of the Panopticon was this "desubjectivized" gaze that could not be pinned down to any particular bearer. A prisoner could not see who saw him, or who talked to him (Bozovic, 1995, 4-11).

Bentham reasoned that the *appearance* of punishment would help to keep the prisoners/labor force healthy and productive, as long as they still felt the terror of punishment. The key to this was omnipresent observation, visible but unverifiable. The power of observation had to be visible in the sense that the prisoner would assume the inspector in the central watchtower was always watching him; unverifiable in the sense that the prisoner did not know if or when he was being watched. He would therefore assume that observation is constant and would exert self-control over his behaviors.[12]

Despite Bentham's 20-year campaign to see its construction, the Panopticon was rejected by the British government, based on the argument that Bentham placed far too much importance on the exploitation of prison labor at the expense of religious reformation (Ignatieff 1978, 109-113). Although the Panopticon never materialized, English penitentiaries in the 19th century did rely on panoptic principles. For example, a regimen of hard labor was institutionalized as a replacement for idleness, which previously reigned in English penitentiaries. Uniforms, walls and bars secured the social distance between the criminals and the outside world. According to Michael Ignatieff, these panoptic principles resonated with the "impartial, humane and vigilant eye of the state, holding the 'deviant' in the thrall of its omniscient gaze" at all times (113).

The Panopticon was taken up by Michel Foucault in his seminal work, *Discipline and Punish* as a way to introduce and illustrate a new theory of power. Foucault argues that the panoptic principle of self-governance renders superfluous the visible devices of surveillance by generating the *disciplinary society*, which he describes as one that observes, retrains and renders obedient the individual instead of punishing him. The Panoptic modality of control focuses its gaze particularly on this population, for it is the deviants who are thought to need self-discipline most and therefore are made subject to systematic surveillance in prisons, hospitals, schools, mental institutions, poorhouses, etc (Foucault 1975).

Many scholars of surveillance theory find the Foucauldian model appealing, but they also point to its inherent problems. One such problem is that this model primarily focuses on 18th and 19th century institutions and cannot be applied to contemporary developments in surveillance. For example, sociologists Richard Ericson and Kevin Haggerty (2000) direct attention to the fact that surveillance is no longer carried out by the State alone, but by several social actors and private individuals who are either directly engaged in surveillance or at least give approval to its practices, which erases the negative connotations found in the Foucauldian model (as well as the Orwellian one). In their "surveillant assemblage" model, Ericson and Haggerty outline a new model of surveillance and social control incorporating the recent technological and social developments into surveillance studies.

In subsequent chapters, I discuss how and in what ways the Panoptic model applies to contemporary video surveillance in public settings. A detailed discussion of recent developments and their implications on theoretical models of understanding video surveillance can also be found in Chapter 5.

A Neutral Technology?

Video surveillance is generally regarded as a safety tool that works in the public interest. Social institutions, public authorities, private entities who champion video surveillance as an effective crime control technology, tell us that its potential negative outcomes – if any – are simply the price we pay for its benefits. This political discourse cements a utopian view of surveillance technology, ignores its negative consequences, and cordons off alternative ways of thinking and talking about surveillance. In this sense, this discourse exemplifies what Herbert Marcuse (1998) refers to as the scientific/technical paradigm adopted by highly rationalized Western societies. Marcuse notes that this paradigm unduly focuses on the efficacy of technology, and translates technological utility into the moral ground from which all human activities are evaluated. Instead, Marcuse suggests, we should assess technology and its human costs from a cultural standpoint (Marcuse 1998, 160-164). A similar criticism of Western societies' social commitment to technology comes from David Noble (1999) who argues that we must undo the myth of the "religion of technology" and not be blind to its limitations. Neil Postman (1983) cautions us to take into account the fact that benefits and deficits of technology are not distributed equally. Postman urges us to ask, from whose point of view is the technological efficiency warranted? What might be its costs? To whom will the technology give greater power, and whose power will be reduced by it? (11) Along these lines, the objective of this book is to assess video surveillance not merely as a technology but as a social, cultural practice, and to pay special attention to its unintended consequences.

One of my epistemological assumptions is that video surveillance programs are not neutral tools that capture reality, but articulations of historical, social and political goals. They facilitate the functioning of social control mechanisms and therefore accrue power to institutions that use them.[13]

Public authorities, local police departments, school administrators and employers argue that they deploy video surveillance to ensure public safety and protect property. Couched in their safety rhetoric, however, lies the attempt to control or alter the behavior of individuals to desired ends. The examination of video surveillance as a manifestation of power arrangements then enables us to shed light on historical, social and political dimensions.

I assert that video surveillance is not merely a technology or a tool for neutral observation or representation of reality. To the contrary, video surveillance is imbued with certain social and political goals, and should be investigated as an articulation of changing alignments of social power and values. Video surveillance is not neutral; it does not represent the real thing. It is indeed a political and normative configuration, because the visual information it extracts from its targets is used as the raw material for decision-making about them. Actors in positions of power record this visual information; they use it as evidence to make decisions about individuals, which will likely affect their life chances. Used in this way, visual information is translated into visual knowledge, the basis for the development of political power. In this sense, video surveillance practices accrue power to the institutional apparatuses of which they are a part. The watchers (government agencies, law enforcement, school administrators, employers, etc.) appropriate video surveillance to expand their power in certain ways. They frame the meanings of video surveillance in ways that are beneficial to them. Furthermore, video surveillance practices help to establish a regime of hierarchical observation. They frame their targets in certain ways. The watched are inside the mise-en-scene, but the watchers remain outside. The watched are visible, but the watchers invisible.

In this context, my understanding of video surveillance is shaped by the work of cultural historian Jonathan Crary. In *Techniques of the Observer* (1990), Crary examines vision and the visual within social and cultural paradigms. Instead of addressing visuality simply in terms of technology and representation, Crary situates the problem of the visual against the backdrop of the reorganization of knowledge and social practices in the first of half of the 19th century, and investigates historically the problems of vision related to the body, the operations of social power, and the institutions and discourse of power.

Crary suggests that a history of vision that sets out to explain the interplay between vision and modernity should not be limited to an investigation of art forms or representation. Crary is critical of historical models that do so. For example, he finds problematic the model that focuses on Impressionism as a rupture from the Renaissance perspective, as well as the model that concentrates on how photography ushered in realism in art. Whether perception or vision changed in the 19th century is not a relevant question, Crary asserts, because perception and vision do not have autonomous histories. The relevant issue is the "plural forces and the rules that compose the field in which perception occurs" (5, 6).

Crary argues that the dependence on the capacities of the human eye for the rationalization of human activity and the standardization of visual imagery have less to do with new ways of mechanized reproduction than they do with broader processes of normalization. For example, the development of the stereoscope, a dominant form for the consumption of photographic imagery in the 19th century, was the outcome of efforts to render the human observer calculable and the human vision measurable and exchangeable.

Drawing from Foucault, Crary notes that the human observer was transformed from "memorable man" to "calculable man," a process in concert with the standardization of visual imagery (17). Therefore Crary suggests that the history of vision and modernity should be concerned with the remaking of the human observer, not the construction or the representation of the external visual object. Crary argues that optical devices should be investigated as part of an effort to extend the human vision and to distance the human observer from what he observes, therefore to make the process of observation standardized and calculable.

In light of Crary's thesis, I approach video surveillance as a technology of vision that generates a new kind of human observer and new practices of observation. I frame video surveillance not merely as a technology that enables human observers to look at something, but as a cultural practice that conditions them to gaze, that is, to see within a set of norms. For example, studies in the United Kingdom show that operators of video surveillance systems in town centers choose to focus on black youth or the poor they associate with wrongdoing or criminal activity, and spend more time watching these groups than white, middle-class men (Norris and Armstrong 1999) or that they disproportionately target Asians and young blacks (Goold 2004). Along these lines, my understanding of video surveillance is that it involves social and cultural prescriptions that guide human observers or system operators to choose what to see and how to see it, and that it leads to certain practices of seeing.

Visual Knowledge and Control

To gain a fuller understanding of video surveillance and the power arrangements of which it is a part, it is necessary to investigate the links between vision, knowledge and control.

Beginning with modernity, visible criteria and observable proof came to be privileged over other forms of information. With the utmost significance attached to visible criteria and the measurability of practically everything in terms of objects and signs, visual experience assumed new roles and vision acquired an unprecedented mobility and exchangeability (Crary 1990, 11, 14). Modern culture invested a functionality in the visual as the primary medium for communication, making it one of the central projects of modernity (Jencks 1995, 2-3).

Aside from privileging sight among the senses and treating it as wholly autonomous, modernity also intertwined seeing and knowing. As Chris Jencks shows, the conflation of visual ability with cognition, of seeing and knowing, of the seen and the known, have led us to begin from visual forms, to talk, theorize and achieve understanding of those forms through mental constructs, and deeply bind up the concept of an idea with the issues of appearance, picture and image.

Further, modern culture also invested in visuality for purposes of observation and documentation. In the 19th century, government inspectors, statisticians, political economists and sociologists vastly increased their efforts to observe and document the wider social and natural environment. As a result, the technical and social apparatus of experimental science developed rapidly, as did a range of disciplines concerned with the observation of social, biological and physical phenomena as they "naturally" occurred (Barry 1995).

With the predominance of visual devices, the act of seeing was considered to be autonomous, that is, severed from the human observer. As Jencks explains, the specialization of optical experience settled into the methodological form of observation, which required the necessity of standing back, of seeing from a distance, the privilege of looking down from an elevated platform. It also established the moral and political authority of the experimental witness, who was considered objective. The observer/witness gained more significance as a means of obtaining knowledge of distant events. But to guarantee the reliability of such knowledge, observation had to be stripped from human emotions; it had to be made rational. Therefore, observation came to rely upon the possession of technical competence and the construction of relatively standardized forms of visual and literary representation (Barry 1995).

As an "agent or instrument that one could believe in as a neutral recorder," observation was ascribed a new meaning as a symbol of order, neutral vision and transparency, all of which coincide with the fundamental traits of modernity (Warner Marien 1997, 39). As material confirmations of the Enlightenment ideals, the optical inventions of the 19th century stressed accuracy, infallible perception and legitimacy. This was a certain and refined accuracy that capitalist modernity generated through the mechanical reproduction of sight, which Crary describes as the "constant re-creation of the conditions of sensory experience" (13).

The dependence on evidence of "nonhuman or inhuman witnesses," in the sense that human capacities are irrelevant to their operation as embodied in the optical instruments (Barry, 43), eventually fostered empiricism and positivism as the methodological strategies that came to dominate modern social theory (Jencks, 46).

Through the increased visibility of data in all fields, observation also came to be used for social ordering, a phenomenon considered beneficial for individual and social progress (Foucault 1977, 148). Foucault directs our attention to the eruption of the new disciplines of psychology, physiology, and rationalization of labor and childcare in the 19th century, all of which strived to make subjects visible and thus controllable. In tandem with processes of modernization and rationalization, ideas about vision were connected to the reshaping of individuals in ways that made them more adequate to the emerging industrial capitalism (Crary, 113). The newly constituted human sciences and the technologies of the self were expressions of the concern with the body and regulating and modifying behaviors.

In his examination of optical devices, Crary points to the translation of the body into a site of knowledge, discipline and truth, "a new continent to be explored, mapped, and mastered" (79). Crary explains that the 19th century excitement and wonderment about the body was due to the assumption that it would be the "basis for the formation of an individual adequate to the productive requirements of economic modernity and for emerging technologies of control and subjection" (81). The central role assumed by optical devices, such as the camera obscura and the stereoscope, had to do with *knowledge and power* that operate directly on the body of the individual" (7). Prior to the socio-economic changes brought forth by capitalism and high-industrialism, attention was something that was external to the human subject. In other words, attention was what the human subject directed at nature, natural phenomena, other human beings or objects. Modernity and its social and economic dimensions changed the concept of attention, and ascribed to it certain functions in the organization and management of education and labor. By the early 20th century, the problem of attention turned from others to the self, mainly for the purposes of productivity and efficiency. Crary argues that the modernist conception of attention is inseparable from the notion of disciplinary institutions. Through the internalization of disciplinary imperatives, the individual is made "directly responsible for his own efficient or profitable utilization within various social arrangements" (1999, 73).

Foucault (1972) also helps to explain the problem of the visibility of bodies, individuals and things under a system of centralized observation. He presents an intriguing sociology of the body, which is of particular concern for him because the body has been seen as a potential source of disorder. Foucault explains that the body is natural and organic, and resists normalization and homogenization. Control of the body together with the control of consciousness, behaviors and relations among individuals is essential to the maintenance of the social order. This is the reason disciplinary power focuses on the body, evaluating it against the norms. The purpose of such normalizing efforts is to return the body to the social order as a productive body.

Therefore, it becomes a matter of obtaining productive service from individuals in their concrete lives. To attain this, power has to be able to gain access to the bodies of individuals, their acts, attitudes and modes of everyday behavior. To be controlled, the body must be seen. Only by keeping bodies under constant surveillance, is it possible to eradicate "darkened spaces" where threats to the social order, such as the "abnormal and the deviant," might emerge. Foucault explains:

> A fear haunted the latter half of the 18th century: the fear of darkened spaces, of the pall of gloom, which prevents the full visibility of things, men, and truths. It sought to break up the patches of darkness that blocked the light, eliminate the shadowy areas of society, demolish the unlit chambers where arbitrary political acts, monarchical caprice, religious superstitions, tyrannical and priestly plots, epidemics and the illusions of ignorance were fomented… The new political and moral order could not be established until these places were eradicated (153).

Based on the workings of the Panoptic prison, which he uses as a metaphor for the all-pervading disciplinary power in modern society, Foucault insists that feeling visible rather than being visible produces the effective social control of individuals, because it makes them become conscious of their visibility (Foucault 1977, 202-203; Reiman 1995, 28). The self-examination by the individual and the subsequent internalized social control is what Foucault describes as "biopower." Biopower is not strict violence or pure coercion, but the interplay of technologies of the self and techniques of discipline (Foucault 1988). What initiates the production of effective social control on individuals then is the *feeling* of visibility and the internalization of the "apparent omnipresence of the inspector."

In considering modernity's reliance on technologized forms of observation and the centrality of these forms to documentation and control, I believe that the photograph can be deemed an early precursor to visual technologies of surveillance.

The history of the photograph reveals how the body of ordinary experience was brought to visibility and thought of in terms of normative order. Suren Lalvani (1996) shows how photographic portraiture in the 19th century became "a disciplinary practice essential to the cultural production of the individual and the family" (59). On the issue of the disciplinary power of the photograph on the self, Lalvani notes that, "social attentiveness and cultural intentionality communicated via the represented body are ideological elements:"

> Photographic portraiture, in confining its production largely to the display of individual males on the one hand and depictions of the cult of domesticity on the other, explicitly modeled and endorsed the symbolic separation between the public and private spheres of bourgeois life (59-60).

Other than endorsing bourgeois values, photography also served as a means of depicting and thus documenting the deviant body. Coupled with the penitentiary, a powerful policing system, and the new science of statistics, photography became a tool in apprehending the criminal, and making the dangerous and laboring classes subjects of surveillance at a time when these lower classes were seen as threats to the expanding capitalist order. Lalvani explains that with the introduction of penal photography in 19th century France, this new way of mechanical reproduction was used for the incarceration of deviant bodies. Thus the body became "permeable to the principle of surveillance", "objectified, divided, analyzed and organized into a cellular structure of space—the file index" (116).

Photographic practices functioned in the cataloguing and apprehending criminals, and also within a group of discourses comprised of criminology, statistics, penology, physiology and eugenics. Paul Knepper and Clive Norris (2009) document in detail how government and police in 19th century used technologies of personal identification, especially fingerprint and photographic techniques to respond to threats of criminality and violence. Christian Parenti (2003) also writes about how the police relied on photography to identify and control deviants and miscreants in the face of the society of strangers created by industrial urbanization and mass immigration in the 19th century. In 1853, for example, the New York City Police Department began photographing repeat offenders and publishing their images in "rogues' galleries." Within the next decade, all major cities from Moscow to San Francisco had opened similar galleries where the public was "invited to call and examine" the images. In addition to identifying the wanted criminals, these galleries functioned as a "ritual of obedience and allegiance to the state" whereby the middle classes could position themselves as law-abiding citizens (38). Susan Sontag (1977) also directs attention to photography as a tool for surveillance and control, when the French police used photographs of Communards to identify and later execute them during the Paris Commune of 1871.

The Privacy Problem

Any examination of surveillance inevitably brings up questions about privacy, and there is much literature on this topic. Scholars concerned with the surveillance/privacy nexus have approached it from the perspective of information technology (and the negative impact of data gathering systems on privacy), privacy regulation and public policy, sociology and political science, and philosophy.[14]

Of these perspectives, I particularly find socio-political and philosophical ones useful. A thorough examination of the privacy problem from a socio-political approach can be found in John Gilliom's insightful book, *Overseers of the Poor: Surveillance, Resistance and the Limits of Privacy* (2001). Here Gilliom criticizes legal approaches to the privacy problem that frame it strictly within the boundaries of privacy rights, and argues that a different assessment is warranted. Gilliom directs attention to the specificity and multiplicity of needs and desires for privacy, and asserts that the way citizens think about rights and laws is not necessarily universal in the same way a privacy discourse that focuses on rights and legal conflict purports it to be. Gilliom writes:

> The ongoing mainstream legal and policy debates about rights to privacy hide specific and substantive needs and desires behind the 'right to be let alone'…and promotes a tendency to ignore the specific and very real relations of power and domination that are at work in policies of surveillance (21).

Gilliom suggests that the current public conversation about surveillance and privacy should shift attention from law and the defense of rights to issues of power and domination. In his investigation of what goes on in the politics of welfare surveillance, how it affects people's lives, and how people struggle with new policies of surveillance, Gilliom focuses less on legal debates and more on the interplay between law, everyday life and individual experience. By paying attention to how low-income mothers from Appalachian Ohio experience welfare bureaucracy and its sustained surveillance system, Gilliom investigates the diverse contexts of pervasive surveillance, its everyday politics, and the personal and political conflicts of people who struggle with it. Instead of assessing surveillance and privacy in the language of lawyers, academics and policymakers, Gilliom listens to the voices and experiences of those who are surveilled and bring them to the forefront.

Informed by this approach to the privacy problem, I explore how individuals experience video surveillance and privacy in the context of everyday life. Aiming to understand the outcomes of video surveillance, I foreground the narratives of park users and students and their constructions of privacy, instead of legal and technical perspectives.

Aside from Gilliom's focus on the context of everyday life, the conceptual framework of this study is informed by Helen Nissenbaum's (2004) and Ruth Gavison's (1980) understanding of privacy. Nissenbaum posits that although general theories of privacy provide significant insights, they overlook context-relative factors, which are of central significance and must be analyzed before establishing whether a particular form of public surveillance (monitoring of individuals in public through video technology or the Internet) leads to privacy invasion. In her theory of contextual integrity, Nissenbaum directs attention to values and norms that govern relationships, practices, and actions in a given context, and notes that these phenomena must be accounted for when assessing privacy invasion claims. For example, while it is appropriate for a physician to request personal health information from his/her patients, the same cannot be said for an employer and his/her employees. In the first context, the collection of such information does not constitute a breach of privacy, but it does in the latter.

Ruth Gavison defines privacy as limitation of other's access to an individual, and suggests that an individual experiences loss of privacy when others obtain information about her, pay attention to her, or gain access to her (428). Gavison acknowledges that neither perfect privacy nor total loss of privacy is desirable. Individuals must be at an intermediate state. They must be accessible to others to a certain extent in order to maintain social relations, and enjoy some privacy to have human activities without the fear of being ridiculed or censured. Gavison directs attention to the positive functions of privacy for both the individual and the society. As it relates to the notion of the individual, privacy restricts physical access, promotes liberty of action, autonomy and human relations; insulates the individual against ridicule and censure, and limits exposure to others. Gavison also notes that privacy contributes to a democratic society because it fosters the moral autonomy of the citizen. It must be noted that Gavison's conceptualization of privacy is not aligned with secrecy or isolation but with autonomy and agency. Gavison maintains that privacy is beneficial to democratic society because it makes it possible for individuals to form judgments and express preferences autonomously, which is central to participation in political decisions. She also notes that privacy is necessary to enable individuals to grow, maintain their mental health, create and maintain human relations, and lead meaningful lives, which are central to a more pluralistic and tolerant society (443-455).

In her discussion of why we value privacy, philosopher Beate Rossler (2005) also argues privacy is essential to leading an autonomous life. "In liberal societies, privacy has the function of permitting and protecting an autonomous life" (1) and "respect for a person's privacy is respect for her as autonomous subject" (117), Rossler contends.

In a similar vein, Daniel Solove (2008) in examining theories of the valuation of privacy, touches upon the respect for each individual's dignity and autonomy. However, Solove directs attention to the difficulty of articulating privacy's value in terms of dignity and autonomy because in some cases, he notes, individual rights may clash: one's autonomy to speak about his/her own experiences can be in conflict with someone else's autonomy to live his/her life without being exposed to others (84-86). Solove also points out to the concept of privacy as a form of protecting personhood. Privacy as personhood is about the protection of the integrity of personality, that is, privacy protects individuality because it protects against conduct that is demeaning to individuality or an affront to personal dignity. Referring to U.S. Supreme Court decisions in *Griswold v. Connecticut* and *Roe v. Wade*, Solove directs attention to how the Court characterized privacy as "an interest in independence making certain kinds of important decisions" especially in matters of marriage, protection, family relationships, contraception, etc. In the meantime, Solove also argues that privacy as personhood is too broad a concept since "our personalities are not purely private" and we readily express in public unique dimensions of the self. Moreover, while one isolated piece of information about an individual is not very revealing, aggregate information can be threatening to personhood or identity (31-33).

Setting the Scene

In this study, I am concerned with experiences of social actors involved in the deployment of video surveillance programs (the watchers) and of individuals who are their targets (the watched). My objective is to present an empirically grounded theoretical framework of video surveillance and its social, cultural dimensions through qualitative research and from the perspective of social constructivist inquiry.[15] Research was conducted in two settings (public park and public school) and mainly focused on interviews with watchers (police officers, school administrators) and the watched (park visitors, students.) Detailed information on research design can be found in following pages.

The key objective of this study is to understand why social institutions turn to video surveillance, and how individuals make sense of video surveillance and privacy in public settings. Accordingly, I ask two broad sets of questions. The first aims to understand the socio-political forces behind the generation and intensification of video surveillance in public spaces. Here I focus on law enforcement, police officers and school administrators, and the primary questions I ask are the following: Why do social institutions turn to video surveillance? What specific objectives do they seek to achieve by using video surveillance? What are the dynamics or trends in the field of crime control, and more broadly social control, that fuel the use of video surveillance in public settings? How does social institutions' concern with risk management affect the use of video surveillance in public settings? What are public authorities' assumptions about the efficacy of video surveillance?

The second set of research questions is concerned with how individuals make sense of video surveillance and privacy in public settings. I focus on park visitors and students—individuals who are indiscriminate targets of the surveillance apparatus by virtue of their presence in the park and the school. By indiscriminate, I mean that these individuals are placed under surveillance as a whole social category or a population group. Indiscriminate video surveillance in the park or the school is not deployed to track a specific person or persons, although in some cases, the watchers might choose to focus on racial, ethnic, socio-economic groups. Indiscriminate video surveillance is rather deployed to surveil the whole population of park visitors and students with the primary objective of deterrence and prevention. In light of the park visitors' and students' lived experiences of indiscriminate surveillance, I try to provoke insight into how they think and talk about surveillance and privacy, and into how they respond to the following questions: How do they experience video surveillance in their everyday lives? What are the meanings they attach to video surveillance and privacy? What are their concerns—if any—about video surveillance and privacy invasion? What aspects of privacy do they evoke in relation to their discussion of surveillance and privacy? What are their conceptualizations of privacy? How do they distinguish between public and private space?

As noted earlier, I conducted empirical research in a public park and two public schools in New York City. I chose the public park as a research site because it is a space that is open to all.[16] Access to the public park is not limited, in the sense that anyone can enter the park grounds and spend as much time in it as he/she wants. To enter the park, one does not have to be affiliated with a given institution or have a specific, demonstrable purpose to be in that space. One is not required to show an ID card or sign in to enter the park. The principle of openness is also demonstrated by the absence of entrances, doors, gates or checkpoints. Further, entry into and the use of public parks is free. One is not required to buy a ticket or make a payment to enter the park nor is required, expected or pressured to engage in any commercial activity during her stay. People generally come to the park for leisurely purposes, to enjoy themselves, spend time with friends, walk their dogs, take their kids to the playground, feed the pigeons, read a book, etc. While they are expected to observe general social rules, they are relatively free from constraints that are usually experienced in other places such as the worksite or the school. And although they are in a public place, they nevertheless expect to be free from prying.

However, the public park is also a space of control. Here I am particularly concerned with control as exemplified by the predominance of regulations that govern the uses of the park, and the increasing policing of parks by law enforcement or private security officers.[17]

While the public park is a space of freedom, it is also a highly regulated space. There are several rules that govern its uses. For example, in New York City parks, people are prohibited from making disturbing noises, camping overnight, possessing alcohol, obstructing sitting areas, spitting, etc. Uses such as bicycling, rollerblading, playing musical instruments, meetings, etc., can take place in designated areas or with a permit.

In this study, within the framework of the coexistence of freedom and regulation in public parks, I examine Washington Square Park in New York City and its video surveillance system, through in-depth interviews with police officers and park users. I interviewed 16 park users in Washington Square Park, between January and May 2004. I also interviewed three police officers from the New York City Police Department. Each interview lasted from 1 to 1.5 hours. Since qualitative researchers do not have to observe a certain quota or a number of interviews, but rather gather meaningful data from participants, I stopped interviewing once the point of redundancy was reached, and I do not think there are any delimitations as to the number of the interviews or the participants. I do not assume that there are any delimitations according to race, gender or socio-economic class. In Washington Square Park, I made sure that the selection of participants reflected these differences. The breakdown of participants in Washington Square Park is as follows: ten women and six men, 14 white and two African-American, 11 middle-class, one upper-class and four working class.

The second research site I chose was the public school. Since the 1990s, an increasing number of schools have deployed video surveillance systems as a means to prevent violent incidents and to maintain discipline among student populations. Proponents of surveillance cameras justify the use of this technology through the claim that video they prevent violence and even help to raise model American citizens. However, critics argue that the presence of cameras worsen students' perceptions of themselves and of their surroundings, and further their sense of themselves as misfits (Dority 1997, Oakes 2000, Monahan 2006).

In this study, I present findings from two public schools in New York City, which I refer to by the pseudonyms, Lincoln Middle School and Jefferson High School. At these schools, I conducted interviews with 13 students and four administrators, between February and June 2003. Each interview lasted from 1 to 1.5 hours. In the schools, my selection of the participants as to race and socio-economic class was prescribed by the composition of student populations; they were predominantly African-American or Hispanic and came from working class families. In addition, I made sure that the selection of participants reflected an equal or close to equal distribution of male and female students. The breakdown of participants at Lincoln Middle School is as follows: four female and two male, three Hispanic and three African-American, two students in 6th grade and four students in 8th grade. The breakdown of participants at Jefferson High School is: four male and three female, six African-Americans and one Hispanic, and seven seniors. Although I wanted to interview the School Safety Agents (SSAs), they declined my requests on the grounds that they are employed by the New York City Police Department and not by the school system, and as NYPD officers they did not deem it appropriate to talk to an "academic" about surveillance.

Outside the schools, I conducted interviews with two high-level officials from the Department of Education, who are engaged in school safety initiatives and the installation and use of surveillance cameras. In addition, I had the chance to interview the Deputy Director and the Executive Director of the Office of School Safety and Planning.

All interviews in the park and the schools were conducted with full confidentiality and upon the participants' active consent. I chose participants based on two primary criteria. First, they should be aware of the presence of surveillance cameras in the given environment (school or park); and second, particularly in the case of Washington Square Park, they should be regular visitors to the park. Participants' awareness of the cameras was especially important, because the idea behind video surveillance is that the power of observation works effectively when the subject knows about the presence of the surveillance system. This is the key theoretical feature of video surveillance as a disciplinarian technology: its existence must be known, yet it must be unverifiable so that the subjects will internalize the uncertainty of the gaze and control their behaviors. The second criteria particularly applied to park visitors in Washington Square Park. It was important to talk to those who came to the park regularly or at least spent a sufficient amount of time in the park so they would have accumulated experiences regarding surveillance cameras.

Following this Introduction, in Chapter 2, I report the results of my analysis of video surveillance practices in public spaces, particularly parks and streets. Chapter 2 begins with the history of the emergence and proliferation of surveillance cameras in these spaces, and examines why video surveillance is being incorporated into crime control and prevention initiatives. This discussion is drawn mainly from in-depth interviews with police officers, and the analysis of press coverage and federal agency and law enforcement reports.

Chapter 3 begins with the history of the escalation of the techno-security apparatus in schools and offers a critical, cultural analysis of video surveillance practices in two New York City public schools. Based on findings from fieldwork in schools and interviews with school administrators and students, I offer insights into the impetus behind school surveillance systems and their *modus operandi*.

In Chapter 4, I turn my attention to the outcomes of video surveillance regarding privacy. Through in-depth interviews with park visitors in Washington Square Park and with students in schools, I explore different conceptualizations of privacy. I explore how and why individuals do not consider video surveillance in public spaces problematic or as an encroachment on privacy. I also pay attention to how the perceived benefits of video surveillance and the sweeping hold of the "I'm not doing anything wrong so I have nothing to worry about" argument calcify the lack of concern for privacy outcomes.

Chapter 5 summarizes the results of the fieldwork, discusses research findings, and presents directions for new ways of theorizing video surveillance that move beyond the Panoptic model.

Notes

[1] "A mom's 'bad day' turns into TV spectacle." *Buffalo News.* September 24, 2002.

[2] For a detailed discussion, see Lyon 2003.

[3] For a detailed discussion, see New York Civil Liberties Union (NYCLU) 2006, Schlosberg and Ozer 2007, National Economic and Social Rights Initiative (NESRI) 2007, American Civil Liberties Union (ACLU) 2008.

[4] See Rule 1973, Laudon 1986, Freedman 1987, Gandy 1989, Linowes 1989, Gandy 1993, Smith 1994, Staples 1997, Whitaker 1999, Garfinkel 2000, Rosen 2001, Lyon 2001, Lyon 2003, Parenti 2003, Solove 2004, Jensen and Draffan 2004, Zureik and Salter 2006.

[5] In contrast to the limited number of scholarly examinations of video surveillance in the U.S. context, one can find several books dedicated to this topic in the United Kingdom. This is mostly because since the 1980s United Kingdom has been the world leader in implementing and operating video surveillance systems in public areas. Criminologists, social theorists and privacy scholars in the U.K. have been acutely interested in video surveillance programs, their origins and effects. In *The Maximum Surveillance Society: The Rise of CCTV* (1999), Clive Norris and Gary Armstrong explore CCTV schemes and social control through extensive fieldwork in three British cities. The collection of essays in *Surveillance, Closed Circuit Television and Social Control* (Norris et. al. 1998) tackles video surveillance in light of social theory, evaluates its deployment, questions its effectiveness, and offers insights into the future. Simon Davies, a leading British scholar in surveillance and privacy studies, discusses video surveillance in several of his works (1996, 1998a, 1998b). In *Policing, Surveillance and Social Control: CCTV and Police Monitoring of Suspects* (2002), Tim Newburn and Stephanie Hayman discuss the use of CCTV in custody cells, and note that CCTV has been accepted by the police and suspects alike for purposes of protection despite its possible intrusion into the "private space" of the cell. Mike McCahill in *The Surveillance Web: The Rise of Visual Surveillance in an English City* (2002) explores video surveillance through its everyday applications in shopping malls, workplaces and housing projects. In *CCTV and Policing: Public Area Surveillance and Police Practices in Britain* (2004), Benjamin J. Goold

investigates the impact of video surveillance on everyday police work. Based on ethnographic research, Goold argues that officers do not rush to integrate this technology into their work; they acknowledge cameras' presence and go about the task of policing as usual.

[6]For more information, visit EPIC's surveillance page at http://www.epic.org/privacy/ surveillance and ACLU's surveillance page at http://www.aclu.org/Privacy/Privacy.cfm? ID=12705&c=39.

[7] For more information on Surveillance Camera Players of New York City and similar groups in other cities, visit http://www.notbored.org/the-scp.html.

[8] To view the maps, visit http://www.appliedautonomy.com/isee.html#maps.

[9] For a detailed discussion, see ACLU. 2008. "What criminologists and others studying cameras have found." June 25. http://www.aclu.org/images /asset _upload_file708_35775.pdf

[10] I use the terms video surveillance and camera surveillance interchangeably. In British literature, the commonly used term is CCTV (Closed Circuit Television), so the reader should understand it as an alternate term for video surveillance or camera surveillance.

[11] Face recognition refers to the integration of video and computer technologies to generate automated facial surveillance. It is a type of biometrics, a method of identifying people based on some aspect of their physical, biological or behavioral characteristics. As Philip Brey (2004) explains, the operation of a face recognition system requires both hardware (video cameras and computer hard drive) and software (a "software engine"). Video cameras view a given space, the boarding area in an airport, for example, and scan the faces of persons within that space. These facial images obtained from the streaming video are then processed by the software engine, which scans them for face recognition. In this process, the software engine compares a facial image against a database or gallery of facial images in order to find a match. It analyzes up to eighty points around the nose, cheekbones and eyes through the use of complex algorithms. Based on the assumption that a facial image consists of a finite number of features unique to each individual, the software engine specifies these features and uses them to distinguish an individual from

others (Bowyer 2004 , Brey, 461). Once the software engine finds a match between a facial image and the database, it alerts the system operator who evaluates the plausibility of the reported match, and takes further action as necessary. Face recognition can be used for authentication, identification or surveillance. As an authentication system, face recognition replaces passwords or PIN's and is used for access control, border control, network and computer security and banking transactions. It associates a given action with the identity of the person conducting it and therefore secures transactions. As an identification system, face recognition compares pictures on ID documents with a database of images of wanted terrorists, criminals, etc in order to detect identity fraud. For example, law enforcement agencies compare mug shots of suspects with criminal databases. As a surveillance system, face recognition is used to detect faces at a distance, in a crowd for example, or to follow the position of a person. In surveillance applications, face recognition systems involve the use of one or more video cameras, which are generally referred to as facecams. Here the purpose is typically to identify criminals, terrorists, missing persons or to track suspicious persons in public places such as airports, casinos, tourist districts (Brey, 459). For a detailed discussion of face recognition and its applications, see Woodward 2001, Lingblom 2003, Lofton 2004. For a discussion of the use of face recognition as part of anti-terrorism efforts, see Gates 2006.

[12] Although Bentham designed the Panopticon as a prison, the principles at work could be expanded to many, if not all, forms of social governance. As he mentioned in the subtitle to *The Panopticon,* this new principle of construction was applicable to "any sort of establishment, in which persons of any description are to be kept under inspection, and in particular to penitentiary houses, prisons, houses of industry, work-houses, poor-houses, manufactories, mad-houses, lazarettos, hospitals and schools." For a more detailed discussion, see Bozovic, 1995.

[13] I would like to thank Allen Feldman for directing my attention to this point.

[14] A detailed discussion of privacy literature can be found in Chapter 4.

[15] Qualitative research attempts to achieve a deep understanding of the social phenomenon in question. It is not concerned with collecting general data from the largest number of persons. It is rather geared towards yielding significant

and meaningful insights. Through a variety of empirical sources, qualitative researchers capture and portray social phenomena that might otherwise go unnoticed. By using multiple data sources, researchers are able to unearth the meanings people make of social phenomena no matter what. As Thomas Lindlof (1995) explains, qualitative research takes social action as its raw material of analysis. Instead of subjecting human behavior to mathematical or other formal transformations, qualitative research seeks to "preserve its form and content and to analyze its qualities" (21). Social constructivism aims to "understand and reconstruct the constructions that people initially hold" (Guba and Lincoln 1998, 211). In other words, it seeks to understand the "complex world of lived experience from the point of view of those who live it" (Schwandt 1998, 221). The main purpose of constructivist inquiry is to understand meanings and definitions attached to social situations by human actors (Schwandt 1998, 221). This is of fundamental significance because it enables researchers to question what's taken for granted and considered obvious and natural. In the public dialogue on surveillance and privacy, it is typically argued that people are disconcerted about surveillance cameras in public spaces and that they think cameras lead to an invasion of privacy. By exploring the meanings people attach to surveillance and privacy, which is called for by social constructivist methodology, I probe these taken for granted assumptions.

[16] Historically, urban parks in the United States have been created to function as pleasure grounds, playgrounds or recreational facilities. As Galen Cranz (1982) explains, in the mid- to late-nineteenth century, urban parks were designed as large, landscaped pleasure grounds located on the edge of a city. They were mid-way between the wildness of pure nature and civilized city life, offering sports activities and mental appreciation of nature. However, because they were far away from the city and required an expensive transit ride, they were not adequately used by the working classes. At the end of the 19th century, the landscaping principles of these pleasure grounds were translated into smaller parks that were closer to the tenement districts and thus more easily accessible by the working classes. In designing these parks, planners were aiming to bring together people, reduce class conflict, and socialize immigrants. The mid 20th century, according to Cranz, is a particular moment in the history of urban parks in the U.S. when parks were simply conceived of as recreational facilities without any social or artistic vision. Since the mid-1960s however, a new model has been in practice, which Cranz refers to as the

Open Space model. This model deems all open spaces as having recreational value and participatory potential. Urban parks have several benefits. In social terms, they are meeting places. They bring together people of all ages and backgrounds and have something to offer everyone. Young children, , teenagers, the elderly, office lunchers, joggers, and dog walkers come to the park and engage in different activities as well as interact with one another. In this sense, parks act as a cohesive force in the community. They also have other benefits such as adding attraction to the neighborhood and acting as an economic asset (Jacobs 1961, 89-111).

[17] In some extreme cases, such as the riots that erupted in Tompkins Square Park in 1988, the phenomenon of control can go as far as the use of force by the police to enforce a curfew in the park. On August 5, 1988, the New York City Police Department evicted everyone from the Tompkins Square Park on the pretext of clearing out the homeless people, buyers and sellers of drugs, and young people playing boom boxes late into the night. In the face of severe public criticism and demonstrations, the police "retreated" that night, but within the next two years they reinstated the curfew, and implemented new regulations governing the uses of the Tompkins Square Park (Smith 1996, 4-5).

CHAPTER 2

Surveillance and the City

Police departments across the nation, in small towns and large cities alike have been using surveillance cameras to deter crime in public spaces, most prominently in streets, parks, public transportation areas and housing projects. In major cities such as Boston, Chicago, Washington D.C. and New York City, cameras are primarily used to prevent terrorist attacks, whereas in others the objective is to reduce crime, crack down on drug trade, deter graffiti and car theft, keep an eye on commuters at busy train stations and on residents in housing projects. Police also use surveillance cameras at traffic lights, intersections and tollbooths to catch toll evaders or drivers who run red lights.[1]

Video surveillance has been used in public places as part of law enforcement's crime control and risk management initiatives for at least three decades now. A March 2001 survey by the International Association of Chiefs of Police found that 80% of U.S. police departments used video surveillance systems in public spaces. At the time the survey was conducted, another 10% planned to install cameras (International Association of Chiefs of Police 2004, 5). According to a study by RAND, also conducted in 2001, 41% of local police departments and 66% of state police departments that participated used fixed-site video surveillance cameras in public spaces (Schwabe 2001, 15). Despite the differences between the two surveys, they both reveal that a considerable number of law enforcement officials use video surveillance. As I will show in the following pages in more detail, video surveillance programs have also been undertaken by urban planners, commercial interests, and public/private partnerships seeking to render public places more secure and thus more profitable.

Law enforcement uses of video surveillance

Objective	*Location*	*Deployed by*	*In partnership with*
Crime prevention, general public safety	Public streets, parks, plazas, transportation areas, housing projects, schools	Law enforcement at local level	Community groups, neighborhood watch groups, BIDs (Business Improvement Districts), housing, education agencies
Homeland security	Public streets, transportation areas, ports of entry, airports	Department of Homeland Security, federal agencies, law enforcement at local, state or federal level	Airports, private businesses
Traffic management	Traffic lights, intersections, highways	Law enforcement at local or state level	

Intensification of Video Surveillance after September 11

Surveillance cameras, which have long been used in crime control and urban renewal projects, are now being repurposed for use in the "war on terror." Fuelled by the technocratic compulsion towards the wider use of surveillance technologies and the misguided belief in their role in preventing terrorist attacks, federal and local authorities have installed new camera systems or expanded existing ones.

Video surveillance networks proliferated remarkably after the events of September 11, both in quantity and quality. According to a 2006 survey, at least 200 towns and cities in 37 states now use video cameras, or are in the process of setting them up, to watch public spaces such as sidewalks, parks, schools, buses, and buildings in response to perceived terrorist threats (Hoffman 2006). Meanwhile, the already existing surveillance programs are growing and becoming more technologically advanced. However, while such proliferation is spurred by anti-terrorism efforts, the primary objective of these new and/or advanced systems remains to be crime prevention.

In Baltimore, for example, the centralized surveillance system, CitiWatch, was created in 2004 with a $1.3 million federal grant, and connected 80 cameras in downtown and Inner Harbor with the existing highway cameras in five counties in Maryland. (Donovan 2004). By 2007, based on anti-terrorism arguments, the system had close to 400 cameras; however these cameras are mostly deployed in downtown tourist areas, high-crime neighborhoods, and five of the city's housing projects. Feeds from cameras, which are equipped with low-light and pan, tilt, zoom capabilities, are monitored by both civilian staff and retired police officers. When they see something suspicious, they can alert the Baltimore police communications center, which then dispatches a police car to the scene. Baltimore police claims that thousands of arrests are made directly based on the video feeds and that crime is down by 15% (Government Security 2007, 19).

The significant increase in the number of video surveillance systems is also examined by American Civil Liberties Union in its survey of 131 jurisdictions in California. According to ACLU, as of 2006, 37 cities in California had video surveillance cameras in public spaces; 18 cities had significant video surveillance programs of public streets and plazas; and additional 10 cities were actively considering similar programs; and 18 cities had systems in which police actively monitor the cameras. Seven of the ten most extensive systems were installed between 2002 and 2006 with federal grants from the Department of Homeland Security.[2]

The availability of funds from the DHS is a significant factor in the escalation of video surveillance in the post-September 11 era. Since 2003, the Department granted millions of dollars to local governments to purchase high-tech surveillance camera networks.[3] In 2007, St. Paul received a $1.2 million grant for 60 cameras for downtown; Madison, Wisconsin bought a 32-camera network with a $388,000 grant; and Pittsburgh added 83 cameras to its downtown surveillance network with a $2.58 million grant. Federal grants also enabled small towns to install cameras in public spaces. Liberty, Kansas (population 95) accepted a federal grant to install a $5,000 camera in its park, and Scottsbluff, Nebraska (population 14,000) used a $180,000 grant to purchase four digital cameras and two monitors (Savage 2007). Philadelphia police initiated a new surveillance program, Operation Safer Streets, with 250 cameras throughout the city, also purchased with grants from the DHS (Clark 2007).

The largest sum of federal money so far has been granted to the New York City Police Department. In 2007, NYPD announced its plans for the creation of the Lower Manhattan Security Initiative, a $90 million blanket surveillance system that resembles London's "Ring of Steel." The extensive web of surveillance, first of its kind in the U.S., is still in the development phase. By the time it is completed, it will include license plate readers, 3,000 public and private cameras in downtown Manhattan, pivoting gates and roadblocks that would automatically shut down a street, and a center to monitor live information (Buckley 2007).

Among other major surveillance projects in New York City is the $20 million electronic security system at Freedom Tower (1 World Trade Center), which upon completion will have not only CCTV cameras but also video analytics, digital recorders, access control systems and a fiber optic network (Dunlap 2008). The Metropolitan Transportation Authority of New York City is also in the process of completing a $212 million surveillance network in the subway system by December 2009. Consisting of 1,000 cameras and 3,000 motion sensors, the network will keep the city's transit system under constant watch, transmitting and recording images from subway platforms, tunnels, bridges, commuter railroads and busy transit hubs like the Grand Central, Penn Station and Times Square (Chan 2005).

New York City is not alone in its surveillance efforts in the face of heightened fear of terrorist attacks. Since September 11, major cities such as Washington D.C. and Chicago have turned to video surveillance, among other technologies, to prevent terrorist attacks at high-profile buildings and structures (Hsu 2002, Kinzer 2004).

The cutting-edge network deployed in Washington, D.C., is perhaps the best illustration of the authorities' penchant for surveillance cameras as "safety tools" in the post-September 11 security zeitgeist. In February 2002, following the latest federal terror alert, Washington police publicly announced that the citywide video surveillance system it had already constructed was fully operational (Bravin 2002, Hsu

2002). The Metropolitan Police Department (MPD) claimed that the system had been used for the first time on September 11, but no further details were made public. What makes this system noteworthy is that its cameras are fully networked and can be centrally monitored. The camera feeds can be viewed by the MPD, FBI and Secret Service from a $7-million command center equipped with 40 video stations angled around a wall of floor-to-ceiling screens. The system also enables law enforcement officials to scan wide stretches of the metropolitan area and create a digital record of images. The system has only 14 digital cameras at places such as the Capitol, the White House, the Washington Monument, Union Station, World Bank and Dupont Circle, but it brings together another 1,000 cameras operated by different agencies, such as the U.S. Park Police, the Department of Transportation, the D.C. school system and the FBI, as well as video feeds from shopping malls, apartment buildings and privately-owned businesses. In justifying the use of surveillance cameras, the project chief Stephen Gaffigan directed attention to the "unique environment [of Washington, D.C.] which needs to be protected." He noted: "In the event of a biochemical or any other event that happens in a subway, a central command officer can actually look in and see what's going on. They can also see inside a school in case of a shooting or hostage incident, manage an evacuation, track a getaway car or perhaps stop a saboteur" (Hsu 2002).

In its "Draft General Order on Closed Circuit Television Cameras" issued in response to requests by privacy advocates and the City Council for the drafting of legislation governing the use of surveillance cameras, the D.C. police insisted that the coordinated system "represents a valid use of the state's power to protect its citizens, and does not intrude upon an individual's sphere of privacy, but rather records events occurring in public space for which individuals do not have a reasonable expectation of privacy" (Metropolitan Police Department, 2002). In March 2002, the D.C. police submitted to the City Council's requests and passed legislation regarding the use of surveillance cameras.[4]

The National Park Service also mounted cameras at the Washington Monument and the Jefferson, Lincoln, Franklin D. Roosevelt, Vietnam Veterans, and Korean War memorials, and in its "Closed Circuit Television Policy" handbook, it asserted that surveillance cameras are used to "help ensure public safety and security, facilitate the detection, investigation, prevention and deterrence of terrorist attacks and crime, help ensure the safety of citizens and officers, help assist in the proper allocation and deployment of law enforcement and public safety resources, and help facilitate the protection of the innocent and the apprehension and prosecution of criminals" (United States Department of Interior 2002). It must be noted that the first time the National Park Service sought to implement video surveillance was immediately after the Oklahoma City bombing in 1995. Terrorist attacks of the scale of those on 9/11 seem to have given the NPS the necessary justification (Hsu 2002).

More recently, the Metropolitan Police Department announced plans to consolidate more than 5,200 cameras operated by city agencies into one network called the Video Interoperability for Public Safety (VIPS). The blanket system, to be managed by the city's Homeland Security and Emergency Management Agency, will allow city agencies such as Public Schools, Housing Authority, Parks and Recreation, Transportation as well as others to share video feeds and enable the police to monitor the system 24/7.[5]

The turn to video surveillance to prevent acts of terrorism is evident in other cities, and is likely to spread. In September 2004, Chicago officials announced plans to add 250 biometrically-enhanced cameras to the already existing 2,000 cameras monitoring public spaces in the city, and to create a 900-mile "Homeland Security Grid" (Spielman 2004). According to Mayor Richard M. Daley and police department officials, the objective of the new system is to make Chicago safer against terrorist attacks and to reduce the crime rate. The system now called Operation Virtual Shield, was completed in 2007, and consists of 2,250 cameras placed by the police and city agencies as well as those owned and operated by private companies. The 250 biometrically-enhanced cameras are placed at buildings and other structures that are considered to be potential terrorist targets. The system incorporates a new advanced software that immediately alerts the police when anyone monitored by the cameras wanders aimlessly or leaves a package behind and walks away from it, allowing them to dispatch officers to the scene if necessary (Jackson 2007). City officials argue that in addition to reducing the crime rate, "the system should be able to make our city safer from a homeland security standpoint." Similar to the system in Washington D.C., the Chicago network brings together cameras used by the police, transit, housing and aviation authorities and by private businesses. Video feeds from all these cameras go to the central control room. A city official said: "The value we gain in public safety far outweighs any perception by the community that this is Big Brother who's watching. The feedback we're getting is that people welcome this. It makes them feel safer" (Kinzer 2004).

In Boston, during the Democratic National Convention in August 2004, the police department installed 30 high-tech cameras near the Fleet Center for fears of terrorist attacks, while the Department of Homeland Security linked approximately 1,000 government-owned cameras with an equally large number of private cameras that monitor the Financial District, City Hall, Downtown Crossing, traffic intersections, and transportation areas. The networking of separate local, state and federal surveillance systems for the first time at a single command post was triggered by public safety concerns emanating from terrorist threats aimed at the convention (as well as the desire to monitor political demonstrators), and law enforcement officials framed the seamless, central monitoring as a one-time happening. However, it became evident that the city-wide surveillance network was not a temporary deployment as various government agencies made provisions to share camera feeds when necessary in the future. Boston police announced that the 30 cameras it installed for the convention would still be used once the convention was over. Police superintendent Robert Dunford said, "We own them now. We're certainly not going to put them in a closet" (Ranalli and Klein 2004).

As above examples show, post-September 11 surveillance systems cull smaller, separate systems together, add new cameras to existing systems and give the law enforcement the ability to create one big monitoring system. This development is not surprising given the fact that in the post-September 11 era the trend has been towards centralization as demonstrated by the consolidation of previously separate information-gathering practices and the creation of the Department of Homeland Security.

Another important dynamic is that video surveillance will certainly escalate even more. By 2008, the list of cities planning to install surveillance cameras grew longer: Richmond, California; Spokane, Washington; Greenville, North Carolina, and San Jose, California all announced plans to add or install surveillance cameras (Vlahos 2008).

Video Surveillance in Historical Context

Although video surveillance systems proliferated drastically since 2001, it would be erroneous to consider them only within the context of the post-September 11 era and as anti-terrorism tools. Video surveillance has been part of a trend in crime prevention that has dominated law enforcement policies and practices in the U.S. since the 1970's. They also have an affinity with "defensive urbanism," a movement that emphasizes security (and surveillance) as design elements that has redefined the field of urban planning. Over the past 20 years, architects, designers, urban planners have been using technologies such as alarm and surveillance systems, and design features such as fortified entrances, walls, gates, checkpoints as part of their projects in order to render the given urban space more protected or defensive against undesired individuals, prominently the poor and the homeless (Ellin 1997).

In the following pages, I provide a critical examination of video surveillance in public spaces through interviews with members of the New York City Police Department and analysis of federal agency and government reports. By contextualizing video surveillance within the frameworks of crime control (and social control, broadly speaking) and urban design, I show why and how video surveillance has come to be defined and accepted as a crime-fighting tool. My objective is to explore the reasons behind the turn to *preventive surveillance* on the part of law enforcement officials and urban planners. I also hope to bring to light the collaboration between public authorities, private corporations and community groups in the "hardening" of the urban landscape and in the privatization of public spaces. I use the term "hardening" to refer to the use of security measures (alarm and surveillance systems, increased policing) and design elements (gates, checkpoints) to make an area more secure or defensible against potential wrongdoers.[6]

Video Surveillance in New York City

In New York City, the police first turned to preventive surveillance in 1973 in Times Square at a time when urban crime rates were at their highest, and the image of the city as a tourist destination was on the verge of total collapse. The objective of the surveillance system was to scan the area for crime, discourage prostitution and muggings and thus make it safer for tourists and businesses. The then-Police Commissioner noted that "every law abiding person who comes to the Times Square area will be delighted to know he is being protected in this way. Only criminals will be worried about being on this television screen" (Schumach 1973). The video surveillance system, which directly or indirectly produced only ten arrests within less than two years, did not fulfill its promise and was quietly abandoned. NYPD offered no explanation as to why the system failed (Cooper 1997). However, the clean-up effort in Times Square was just beginning, and the use of video surveillance as a crime-fighting tool was about to become commonplace in New York City and across the nation.

From the 1980s onwards, attempts to harden public spaces (that is, render them protected or defensive against unsavory, threatening people and behaviors) by using video surveillance as a preventive measure became more systematic. Police departments directed attention towards housing projects, public transport, parks, streets and schools, and added surveillance cameras to the already existing mix of preventive measures (increased patrolling, fortified entrances, and checkpoints) to render them safe. NYPD undertook an extensive installation of surveillance cameras to deter crime at subway stations, among other places.

The first large-scale system, with 76 cameras, was placed at the Columbus Circle station in 1981 with the intention of "giving the cops an extra pair of eyes." However, the system, which came with a price tag of $500,000, did not cut down crime as expected. On the contrary, crime rose by 30% at that station, an increase that officials were unable to explain. Two years later, unfazed by this failure, the Metropolitan Transit Authority (MTA) mounted 136 cameras at the Times Square station (Goldman 1983). It is not known whether the camera system helped in apprehension of criminals. Today, there are cameras at almost every subway station in New York City, and they are usually trained on hallways, passageways, ticket booths and tracks to monitor criminal activity and act as a deterrent. After September 11, 12 digital cameras were installed at Grand Central terminal. New York City Transit has also been considering the installation of cameras on buses and subway trains to prevent crime, vandalism and assaults on drivers, framing the surveillance system as an anti-terror measure (Skenazy 2004).

In the mid- to late nineties, surveillance cameras proliferated across New York City as part of Mayor Rudy Giuliani's war on crime. In October 1996, Guiliani and Police Commissioner Safir announced plans to install cameras in Central Park and subway stations. Inspired by a similar effort in London, England, Safir was adamant that video surveillance would offer law enforcement officials "a low-cost way to monitor activities without expanding the size of the [police] department" and that "the benefits of cameras in solving and deterring crime would far outweigh any potential of [privacy] intrusion" (Kocieniewski 1996). As part of this crime prevention program, that same year 39 cameras were installed in Grant Houses, a public housing project in Harlem. Eight other housing projects soon followed. Guiliani credited the surveillance system in these housing projects with a reduction in serious crime of more than 20% (Kennedy 1997).

Although these statistics were not methodologically sound because they did not take into account the effect of displacement factor which the NYPD's Legal Bureau admitted (Chou 2000), law enforcement officials nevertheless talked them up as success stories to justify the expansion of video surveillance systems to other public spaces, most prominently streets, sidewalks, buildings and parks. In regard to this and similar studies that proclaim surveillance cameras as effective in reducing crime, it must be remembered that research can be skewed, neglecting the fact that cameras generally displace crime to immediately adjacent or larger areas, rather than prevent it.

Prominent Video Surveillance Deployments in New York City

Year of installation	*Location*	*Number of cameras*
1981	Columbus Circle subway station	76
1983	Times Square subway station	136
1996	Grant Houses (housing project)	39

The above table spotlights milestones regarding the deployment of video surveillance systems in New York City. Two points need to be made regarding this table. First, it includes surveillance systems owned and operated only by the NYPD. It does not include systems deployed by private entities such as retail businesses, restaurants, office buildings and parking garages. It is estimated that the total number of privately owned cameras in NYC, trained on public streets, is more than the number of police cameras.[7] Second, video surveillance systems mentioned in this table mostly consist of what is known as "first-generation" cameras. These cameras are fixed in position, with no pan, tilt or zoom features. Second-generation cameras, which are fast replacing their predecessors, can pan 360° degrees, have superior lenses, and are better protected against vandalism. Their lenses are hidden in what looks like black snowballs, and often times they are not recognized as cameras. Also, since they have increased zoom and focus capabilities, they don't need to be deployed in great numbers. Law enforcement and security companies generally mislead the public by arguing that the number of cameras in a given place is not that many, therefore there is no reason to worry about privacy invasion. However, they fail to mention the fact that these cameras are second-generation and have remarkably more viewing capacity than their first-generation counterparts.

In its 1998 survey, the New York Civil Liberties Union identified 2,380 cameras trained on public spaces in NYC (owned by both NYPD and private entities) (Lambert 1998, Goodnough 1998). By 2006, there was a significant increase in the number of cameras. As the below table shows, in some areas the increase *is* astounding. Although it doesn't include a survey of all the boroughs or neighborhoods but a few select ones, the NYCLU study nonetheless opens our eyes to the creation of a massive surveillance infrastructure.[8]

Neighborhood Cameras in New York City as of 2006

	1998	*2006*
Financial District, Tribeca	446	1306
Greenwich Village, Soho	142	2227
Lower East Side, Chinatown	181	643
Central Harlem	NA	292
Total	769	4468

Video Surveillance in Washington Square Park

Following this brief background information on the emergence and proliferation of video surveillance in public spaces, I now turn my attention to the surveillance system in Washington Square Park. In light of interviews with NYPD officers and park visitors, I explore the impetus behind the deployment of surveillance cameras, their everyday workings and unintended consequences such as displacement of crime.

Washington Square Park is a hub of activity in the heart of Greenwich Village. Located in a residential area and in natural vicinity to New York University and coffee shops, clubs and stores on Bleecker and Macdougal streets, the park is a popular spot. Its facilities—playgrounds, chess player's area, and the dog run attract people of all ages and backgrounds; and the central fountain basin is, in the words of Jane Jacobs (1961), "a theater in the round" for performers and spectators (105).

In 1960s, the park was popularized by beatniks as a hangout spot and became a favorite of Village residents for its peaceful, bohemian ambiance. But it became derelict during the mid-sixties. Park Commissioner Robert Moses proposed plans to redesign the park, which were met with criticism by West Village residents, led by Jane Jacobs. Jacobs and others opposed Moses' plans to have a major depressed highway cut through the center of the park. Eventually

Moses abandoned his plans and the park was closed to traffic in 1971 (Jacobs 1961, 360). Although it briefly enjoyed the fruits of its renovation, the park became a center for drug dealing in the 1980s, mostly as result of the urban decay of the previous decade. In the 1990s, the Guiliani administration aimed to reclaim the park through police crackdown and the use of video surveillance cameras, and succeeded to do so, according to many.

Today, Washington Square Park, in the words of a Greenwich Village resident who is a regular visitor, is a "nice place to enjoy some peace and quiet in the middle of the city." On most days, the park buzzes with activity. Parents, babysitters and children crowd the playground; office workers escape their cubicles for lunch breaks on benches; and tourists cheerfully pose for the photographs under the famous arch. In spring and fall, the central fountain becomes a performance space for street entertainers, and students from the neighboring university lie on the grass and sunbathe.[9] One can always find a few folks playing musical instruments and chess players immersed in spirited games surrounded by impromptu audiences. Amidst all this, drug dealers move around the main pathways of the park mumbling "trees, trees" or "smoke" to passers-by. According to a police officer, the level of dealing is much lower than during the 1990's, but the "drug problem" still exists in Washington Square Park (author's interview).

In the following section, I draw on interviews with three NYPD officers from the local precinct and explain the underlying reasons as to why law enforcement turned to surveillance technology to deal with drug trafficking in Washington Square Park. Also, in light of interviews with sixteen park visitors, I offer a critical examination of the surveillance system in Washington Square Park.

In the 1990s, according to Lt. Matthews,[10] the drug problem in the park was so bad that the police and the community decided to "step up" and "get a handle on it." First, the police placed a permanent officer in the park that people could report dealers to. However, faced with "geographic" challenges the park presented in terms of effective policing, they "switched to cameras." In the words of another officer, Sgt. Evans,

> Washington Square Park is 15 acres. It is much more difficult to [monitor] than it would be on a small street like Grove Street. So you could certainly have a number of officers on one side of the park, but [the drug dealers] could be dealing anything they like on the other side. It is very hard to police. There are trees; there are places to hide.

Determined to "clean up" the park and the neighborhood, and clear it of drug dealers, the NYPD, under the instruction of the Mayor's office, placed two surveillance cameras in Washington Square Park and a police van on the southeast corner of the park where officers could screen the camera footage. The surveillance system quickly expanded to include a dozen cameras within a matter of a few years (Ravo 1998). In June 2004, the police replaced the old analog cameras with digital ones to provide higher resolution images, rather than "grainy pictures" (author's interview). Digital cameras have a 360-degree scope and can zoom in close enough to see if people are exchanging drugs and money (Hope 2004).

On the day the surveillance system was announced to the public (also the same day it had been deployed, according to the police) Police Commissioner Howard Safir held a press briefing in the park to proclaim that the "drug traffickers have left the park, and we assume that as we put more cameras up they will continue to keep the park free of drug traffickers and have it for what it was meant for, for the families and citizens of this city" (Lee 1998). In the following days, the American Civil Liberties Union (ACLU) harshly criticized the surveillance system arguing it led to privacy invasion. A handful of protestors condemned it for encroaching on the Fourth Amendment. Yet many residents of Greenwich Village welcomed the cameras, assuming they would "clean" the park of drug dealers. NYPD told one success story after another about how the cameras helped them "catch criminals." A police officer interviewed for this study argued that over a period of years, the more overt drug dealing did indeed wane.

However, the effect of surveillance cameras in terms of crime reduction is not that clear-cut. Law enforcement officials and community residents (at least some of them) believe that the park is largely drug-free and much safer thanks to the surveillance system. According to the community affairs officer of the local precinct, Sgt. Dillon, people living in the neighborhood are in favor of the cameras:

> The block associations that surround the park or the parents that they take their children to the children's playground say that it's better. And that shows that [cameras] work. We go by the feedback we get from the community.

Remarks made by park visitors support this point. For example, Anita, a white woman in her fifties who lived in the neighborhood since 1986 and is a regular in Washington Square Park, observes that the park is safer thanks to increased policing and surveillance:

> In the eighties and nineties, I remember I couldn't walk through the park without people approaching me to try to sell me drugs. That's just the way it was. There were more homeless people in the park. People were aggressive. Panhandlers were a little more aggressive. People would come up to you and stuff.

In a similar vein, Jane, a mother in her early thirties who visits the park with her young daughter adds that surveillance is a good thing:

> I have to say that the Guiliani administration did fabulously to cut crime in city life in general, but in Greenwich Village it's just really been a huge difference. It made the city a place I love to be that I want to raise my daughter in. And I think [surveillance] is a contributing factor. It helps keep things safer, makes people happier, makes people want to live here. And if it promotes a sense of safety whether it's actually causing safety or not, I think if people feel better about it, it's a good thing. It makes you feel safer.

In comparison to the local residents' positive feelings, those who come to the park from other neighborhoods tend to offer different views. For example, Paddy, a student in her twenties who lives in Brooklyn and comes to the park to meet with her friends, is more critical of the surveillance system in Washington Square Park and other public settings:

> To me it's more of a scare tactic by the police. To stop people from doing things. And if somebody actually did something to me I would rather have a policeman right around the corner able to run and catch the guy than a camera to [capture it on] record. The record down the road might help, but I think that it is more effective to have [police officers] walking around.

Jim, a white, middle-class male who comes to the park for his lunch break echoes this implicit criticism of the assumption that cameras can prevent or cut crime:

> Cameras exist but there are still crimes and there are still people doing dumb things. It's not going to completely diminish that, but it all depends on… I think if you have the intent to do something, you'll probably do it regardless of the cameras. That's what you're setting out to do. So I don't really think that [cameras are] going to make that much of a difference.

Another park visitor, Monica, an African-American woman in her fifties who comes to the park for play dates for the toddler she babysits, comments:

> Even though there are security cameras there…still…when it's dark and there are lots of trees and benches and things that people can be behind. It's well lit but it's still nighttime, you just never know who is in the park. There's no way to keep people out, there's no way to…you never know what could happen. They could still jump you, grab your wallet and run away. Somebody would see it obviously on the security camera but the reaction time and all that stuff…it can still happen.

Indeed, Lt. Matthews acknowledged the fact that cameras do not reduce or eliminate crime, but rather displace it:

> The local drug dealers, they know where [the camera] is. Sometimes they look at the camera…they know where it's

> pointed. If they want to do a drug deal, they'll go to a certain area of the park that might not be covered, might have the trees in the way. They're not stupid either.

The displacement factor is actually what led the NYPD to add more cameras to the park and even install them on surrounding streets. As Lt. Matthews told me:

> Initially cameras were just in the park itself. Then we added another one on 6th Avenue and West 3rd Street and then another one on 6th Avenue and West 4th Street, because a lot of the drug activity moved onto 6th Avenue after the cameras were installed [in the park]... There is a decrease in the number of arrests in Washington Square Park, but there has been an increase in arrests around the park because [drug dealers] move to different areas.

Sgt. Dillon, the community affairs officer, also admitted that the "drug condition is not gone." When asked if this is an indication of the failure of the surveillance scheme, he argued that it is not about cameras but the criminal justice system itself:

> The amount of drugs [bought and sold in the park], especially if it's marijuana, is very small. And that's why the majority of the judges really don't take it very seriously. For practical purposes, it's been decriminalized by the courts. So [dealers] aren't afraid to be arrested. They're probably going to do 24 hours or less in jail. And for them it's part of doing business if they are a drug dealer, you have to get arrested every once in a while.

Sgt. Evans made a similar point:

> The repeat offenders... you see, some of these guys get locked up, they get 40, 50 arrests for doing it. But apparently if they're only getting grabbed once every two or three months, for them it's the price of doing business. Okay, I'm making money today, then I'm going to have to go to jail for two days and I'll have to pay a fine, okay...like rent. Then

> you're back out and you're doing it again. They have that leeway with the courts, and there's no place to put them anyway. You can't put these minor drug offenders in jail.

Despite all these factors that undercut the effectiveness of the surveillance system, these three officers nevertheless tended to portray the cameras as successful. Statements to the effect that the "volume of people selling drugs in the park has decreased a lot," or that the "drug problem certainly isn't as bad as it used to be," were offered in defense of the surveillance apparatus. In addition, they noted, even if the cameras did not eradicate drug trafficking, the police still find them helpful in other investigations and for gathering evidence. Sgt. Evans said:

> A lot of times people don't believe you when you say, well this guy sold drugs here. Well, how do you know? I saw it on tape, here's the tape. Then the trial lasts about 30 seconds. All I have to do is take that tape in the courtroom and the jury would watch it and there'd be no problem.

Lt. Matthews echoed:

> People say they get robbed in the park. But then we [look at] the video and they were lying. They were going to buy drugs or they were drug dealers and the guy said I was thrown on the floor and the guy pulled a knife on me. And [we] looked at the tape, and you see him…nothing happened to him.

Such uses of surveillance footage are not unusual. The International Association of Chiefs of Police survey shows that 63% of the police departments who use video surveillance find it useful for investigative assistance, with 54% using it for evidence gathering (International Association of Chiefs of Police 2004). However, the primary—and apparently somewhat naïve—goal of video surveillance remains *prevention*. As Sgt. Dillon told me:

> What a lot of people don't understand is that the cameras aren't put in the park to catch drug dealers. They are put in the park to *deter* drug dealers. To get all of the dealers out of the park: that's what their purpose is.

And since the underlying reason is to deter dealers by letting them know that they are being watched,

> There was a lot of publicity when the cameras were installed [in the park]. They weren't put up in secret. It was in all of the regular city papers, and all of the local papers. We absolutely wanted people to know that there were cameras. That was all part of the plan.

Park visitors' constructions resonated with these comments regarding the preventive effect of the surveillance system. Jim said:

> I would say if you're a criminal or something like that you probably soon find out that there was a surveillance system. I think it's a deterrent. Absolutely. A deterrent to crime. And it's a good safety measure. I think it's a nice safety measure. I like it.

Jane's remarks echoed this sentiment:

> I assume that people think twice about doing anything that can be construed criminally, that somebody could come back and say, "Hey we just caught you and we have it on tape.

Why then is video surveillance used as a deterrent? What are the factors that inform law enforcement's thinking regarding video surveillance? What is the reasoning behind the use of video surveillance? To answer these questions, it is necessary to examine video surveillance not as a technology but as a social practice, prompted by certain developments in crime control and urban design, and situate it within the framework of risk society.

Preventive Surveillance and Crime Control

The deployment of surveillance cameras in public spaces is representative of new approaches in crime control and urban design that came to shape law enforcement and urban planners' response to crime since the 1970s. The idealistic rehabilitation programs predominant in the previous decade, which aimed to treat criminals and return them to society as law-abiding citizens, had fallen out of favor by the 1970s. Criminologists and sociologists turned their attention to new models of crime control. In stark contrast to prior approaches that focused on moral reformation and the mind as the site of discipline (based on Bentham's philosophy), the new model of prevention sought to change the physical and social structures in which individuals may commit offensive and illegal acts.

The preventive model views crime not as an individual deviance that requires moral reformation, but as a set of risks that can be prevented by means of creating defensible spaces, hardening targets, and investing in hardware and preventive technologies. As sociologist Stan Cohen (1985) observes, the preventive model emphasizes:

> [T]he control of whole groups, populations and environments—not community control, but the control of communities. In this movement, technology and resources, particularly at the hard end, are to be directed to surveillance, prevention and control, not "tracking" the individual adjudicated offender, but preventive surveillance (through closed-circuit television, for example) of people and spaces (127).

Cohen argues that this new strategy of prevention is borne of the "master shift" in social control that has been ongoing since the mid-20th century. It is concerned with the identification, classification and management of dangerous populations with the intention of "regulat[ing] groups as part of a strategy of managing danger." It directs power towards prevention and risk minimization that targets "the population itself, in its biological and demographic sense" (Feely and Simon 1994, 173, 177).

This new approach was adopted by law enforcement officials in the early 1970s. As part of their efforts to prevent crime, or at least alleviate fear of crime, they began directing attention to greater control of the physical environment by resorting to technological resources, most prominently alarm systems and surveillance cameras (Cohen 1983, Garland 2001). Alarm systems and surveillance cameras are similar in the sense that they both embody preventive rationalities. In deploying these technologies, law enforcement tells people to watch what they do: unlawful acts or wrongdoing will lead to alarms going off or will be captured on video. However, there is a difference between alarm and surveillance technologies. Alarm systems do not produce any records but surveillance systems do, and are therefore considered more effective in deterrence and prevention.

Risk Society and Video Surveillance

In their discussion of how surveillance and security displace traditional crime control policies, Ericson and Haggerty (1997) note that in modern society there is less concern with labeling of deviants as outsiders and more concern with developing a risk-profile knowledge of ordinary individuals (18). They direct attention to the relationship between surveillance and risk management, and situate surveillance as part of risk society.

Although Foucauldian concepts of discipline and control are still prevalent, contemporary society is to a greater extent defined as "risk society" (Simon 1987) or "post-disciplinary order" (Castel 1991), where the "primary aim is not to confront a concrete dangerous situation, but to anticipate all the possible forms of eruption of danger" (288). Since risk is not borne out of concrete subjects but from "a range of abstract factors," and risk society is driven by the distribution of "bads" and "dangers" as opposed to "goods," power in risk society is persistently aimed at prevention (Beck 1992, 49).

In risk society, Ulrich Beck (1992) notes, experience and action in the present are not determined by the past but the future, by something "non-existent, invented, fictive" (34). This is why risk society is "particularly negative and defensive" where "one is no longer concerned with obtaining something 'good,' but rather with preventing the worst; and self-limitation is the goal which emerges" (49). In risk society, non-existent, future "bads" can emerge not merely from the deviant but from anyone and everyone, therefore concerns over security displace the traditional focus on deviance and the labeling of deviants as outsiders. This produces a corresponding shift in emphasis towards the development of a risk-profile knowledge of individuals in order to "ascertain and manage their place in institutions" (Ericson and Haggerty 1997, 18). Therefore, in risk society, preventive strategies promote a "new mode of surveillance" that is no longer concerned with individuals, but with flows of populations that are likely to produce risk (Castel 1991, 288). As Ericson and Haggerty note,

> Risk society is fuelled by surveillance, by the routine production of knowledge of populations useful for their administration. Surveillance provides biopower, the power to make biographical profiles of human populations to determine what is probable and possible for them. Surveillance fabricates people around institutionally established norms—risk is always somewhere on the continuum of imprecise normality. These norms are never static. They emerge from the inter-institutional politics of risk in which rules for classifying populations are negotiated... Surveillance is systemic, providing both the condition and the product of an institutions' knowledge of itself and of other institutions. Surveillance bolsters bureaucracy, helping it to form its authority and govern at a distance (450).

Leading surveillance studies scholar David Lyon (2001, 2007) also notes that surveillance systems expand as a result of the modern society's desire to reduce uncertainties and control outcomes. To manage risks or to "administer populations in relation to risk," institutions, agencies and organizations keep track of individuals' daily activities not only as workers but also as consumers and citizens. In contemporary societies, Lyon argues, surveillance is a "central means of social ordering or social orchestration" in order to classify, coordinate and control populations. It is the means of risk management and of obtaining compliance and containing threatening behavior through the production of knowledge about individuals (2001, 6-10).

The idea of "governing at a distance" through surveillance and other risk management techniques can also be traced to the changing role of governments in provision of public services. Neo-liberal regimes of the late 20th century invented "new strategies of government" to overcome their failures and achieve their objectives such as reducing costs of public services, dealing with problems of welfare, undercutting the power of professional lobbies (Rose 1996, 53). Among these new strategies of governing are the proliferation of quasi-autonomous non-governmental organizations taking on responsibilities for the provision of public services, the replacement of the social citizen and their common society with the responsible individual and their self-governing community, and the devolving of responsibility for health, wealth and happiness to "non-political" apparatuses such as schools, hospitals or private businesses (55, 56).

Similar to other fields, in crime control, governments find themselves compelled to cut down spending and ask the citizenry to take more responsibility to reduce crime, particularly by being cautious, and by avoiding risk and victimization. They seek to "devolve responsibility for crime prevention onto agencies, organizations and individuals which are quite outside the state and to persuade them to act appropriately" while making sure that they did not make their own decisions about risk management and act as local militia (Garland 1996, 451).

In light of these perspectives, it can be argued that in contemporary society, individuals are encouraged to monitor their behaviors, shun inappropriate, unwanted, unreasonable acts, and take responsibility for themselves, their loved ones and communities by using surveillance cameras or by giving consent to public/private entities that deploy cameras. Therefore, through video surveillance, contemporary, neo-liberal society attempts to establish continuous, permanent, and effective governing of the populace at a distance. In this sense, video surveillance resonates with a particular mode of governance that Foucault conceptualizes as governmentality. A detailed discussion of how governmentality helps us understand contemporary video surveillance can be found in Chapter 5.

Urban Design and Video Surveillance

To understand the "camerafication" of public spaces, the turn to video surveillance must be situated within the framework of urban design as well as crime control. Since the 1970s, and in parallel with law enforcement's emphasis on prevention, urban planners and environmental designers have been incorporating video surveillance into their projects. Of course, changes in urban design ignited by crime and the fear of it are not specific to the late 20th century. Such changes can be traced back to the late 18th and early 19th centuries.

Transformations in city design stemming from fear of crime materialized with the transition from feudalism to capitalism, and as the accelerated changes brought about by modern industrialization began to incite insecurities among the bourgeoisie. The "unreliable and often sub-standard working conditions of the new wage-earning class, the inherent antagonism between it and the small class of owners, [and] increased geographic mobility due to the unrelenting search by people for better wages and by workplaces for greater profits" created a "new constellation of fear... both within the factory and outside of it" (Ellin 1997, 20).

To cope with such fears certain mechanisms were put into operation, exemplified by Taylor's scientific management inside the factory and the imposition of the grid for urban development outside it. The most famous example of such a transformation is the redesign of Paris between 1853 and 1872, overseen by Baron Haussmann and the Emperor Napoleon III. Haussmann sought to clear slums, which he regarded as "unhealthy islands," and open up "breathing spaces" in the city. Central to the redevelopment of Paris was standardization, thus giving the city a sense of order. The underlying purpose of such city design was to "bring about social reform, especially by instilling morals and the work ethic." By suppressing the social and productive activities in favor of movement and consumption, the public space was rationalized and commodified (18, 20).

Since the 19th century, the culture of fear has transformed public spaces into guarded and controlled places (although not always successfully); increased the visibility of the ruled but decreased the visibility of the rulers; and created disciplinary spaces (34-35).

In late 20th century, the pressure to reduce crime and alleviate fear of crime directed urban planners' attention to the creation of disciplinary spaces. Planners established that environmental factors were instrumental in the commission of crimes, and believed that if such factors could be manipulated then crime could be prevented. This movement in urban design manifested itself in the form of two related approaches: Crime Prevention through Environmental Design (CPTED) and "defensible space."

Urban planners together with housing authorities and security experts have incorporated both these approaches into their practice and continue to do so. Indeed, research for "defensible space" was conducted in New York City housing projects, and later on it was adopted by the New York City Department of Housing. Today references to these approaches can be found in security industry publications and in National Institute of Justice research reports (Smith 1996, Taylor 1995).

CPTED was developed by C. Ray Jeffrey in the early 1970s as a response to the inability of existing crime control models to tackle increasing crime rates. Illustrative of the new approach to crime control that Cohen describes, CPTED shifts the emphasis from the punishment or treatment of the offender to the control of the physical environment and the behavior of people within it (Jeffrey 1971). Jeffrey argues that the rehabilitative model, which aspires to educate delinquents, is a failure since it deals with the "individual offender after" the crime has been committed (79). Instead, Jeffrey maintains, a successful crime control model "must deal with behavior before the crime occurs, must deal directly with criminal behavior, and must deal with environmental design, rather than the individual offender" (278). To this end, CPTED emphasizes the use of alarm systems, surveillance systems, and community involvement, which Jeffrey believes will create a physical environment that will deter the criminal from committing a crime.

The second approach, one that is closely related to CPTED, is "defensible space." Developed in the 1970s by architect Oscar Newman of the Institute for Community Design Analysis and a proponent of CPTED, "defensible space" aims to prevent crime by means of introducing changes in the built environment.

Newman (1972) suggests that the "manipulation of building and spatial configurations" creates a defensible space, deters criminal activity, and contributes to a secure environment. Defensible space seeks to bring an environment under the control of its residents and amplify their "ability… to casually and continually survey their environment" through various real and symbolic barriers, strongly defined areas of influence, and increased and improved opportunities for surveillance (50). The approach also highlights citizen participation and community involvement in tackling crime by creating a "commonly shared effort" among habitants to maintain the physical environment and discourage non-inhabitants from using that space (206).

However, it must be remembered that, as holistic approaches to security, both CPTED and "defensible space" are designed to prevent property crimes (vandalism, theft, trespassing), and not crimes against a person (assault, harassment), interpersonal or premeditated crimes. Further, as in the case of video surveillance, a technique common to CPTED and defensible space, critics argue that the risk management mentality is "not to get rid of crime but to make it someone else's problem" (Rentschler 2003, 250).

Remarks made by Sgt. Dillon in reference to the surveillance system in Washington Square Park illustrate this point:

> As you move the drug dealers out of the park, they're not just going to disappear. They're going to go to other areas. There's an increase just on the other side of Houston Street, which is [another] police precinct. When we looked at the names of people being arrested down there, it was the same marijuana dealers that used to be in the park. They moved a few blocks away. Their customers found out where they were. They do the dealing there.

Despite such shortcomings, urban planners, designers, developers and police departments have used and continue to use video surveillance and other preventive measures to render public spaces defensible.

One of the important factors that contribute to this phenomenon has been the institutionalization of crime and crime consciousness in urban planning and environmental design. Since the 1980s, this predilection for security at the expense of urban reform and social integration has resulted in the "armoring" of cities and the hardening of the urban landscape.

Defensive and preventive measures in urban design include, but are not limited to: the active monitoring of a public space by roving patrols and/or surveillance technologies; defending a space by wall-mounted sprinkler heads activated to clear loiterers or ledges sloped to inhibit sitting; obscuring a public space by view impediments such as intervening objects or grade changes; contorting or protracting paths of approach to a public space; and obstructing access by walls, gates, checkpoints (Flusty 1997, 48-52).

Planners have also utilized more innocuous measures in urban centers to tackle crime, or at least alleviate the fear of it. In Dallas, Minneapolis, Montreal and Charlotte, underground and overhead walkways and tunnels have been built between public transport areas, malls and business complexes in order to cocoon middle-class pedestrians from the perceived dangers of downtown streets (Boddy 1992).

In his observations of Los Angeles, Mike Davis (1992) notes how the obsession with security, CPTED and defensible space triggered the use of "bumproof" benches at bus stops to prevent homeless people sleeping on them, the bulldozing of public toilets, and the aggressive deployment of outdoor sprinklers to discourage the homeless from sleeping in public parks. While these defensive tactics (defensive in the sense that they aim to *defend* the given space against particular groups of people) have made the public spaces of Los Angeles unlivable for the homeless and the poor, they have made them safer and more attractive for businesses, restaurants and their middle-class citizen consumers, Davis argues (160-163).[11]

In addition to protecting middle-class consumers in urban centers, surveillance and associated defensive programs also aim to protect business districts and corporate interests.[12] The main objective of these security measures, and the larger urban renewal projects of which they are part of, is to maintain property values in the gentrified enclaves of inner cities and profits in the malls, restaurants and cultural centers of downtown areas. Architects, planners and designers, driven by the prospect of the profitable operation of these commercial spaces, incorporate surveillance measures into their designs as part of what Nicholas Fyfe and Jon Bannister refer to as the "fortress impulse" (1998, 254, 255).

Seen in this light, it makes sense why in New York City for example there are many more surveillance cameras in the Wall Street area than in Harlem. According to a 1998 report by the New York Civil Liberties Union, the financial district and midtown Manhattan, as homes to a multitude of corporations, are the most heavily watched areas in New York City (Lambert 1998).

The link between surveillance systems and the protection of commercial, corporate interests was also observed by two park visitors in this study. Paddy said,

> If you look at public places, it's places with more affluence that have cameras. Places around certain buildings like in Wall Street, they have certain places with cameras and stuff. It's just places where you find a lot of money, where you find the cameras.

Meanwhile, Tom, an African-American man who said he lives in a poor neighborhood in Brooklyn but comes to Washington Square Park to play chess with his friends noted,

> We don't have cameras in my neighborhood. But here [in Greenwich Village], there's a lot of money around here. And when I say that, we're talking about one of the top 5 colleges in the country. New York University. People pay a lot of money for their kids to go to school here.

Band Aid solution?

While Paddy and Tom referred to corporate concerns, others pointed to the feel-good factor cameras create and politicians' desire for quick fixes to social problems. Jim directed attention to how people, especially those who harbor unsubstantiated fears, get a feeling of safety from the cameras:

> Some people are so scared of everything. So they think that if they have a camera in a public place it's going to somehow prevent them from being mugged or attacked or something. I think it's more of an image kind of thing. People feel safer having the cameras; they feel better.

According to Kaitlin, a white woman who comes to Washington Square Park during her lunch break, the turn to surveillance cameras symbolized a "band aid" solution to "big problems:"

> They don't go to the source of the problem; they go to the symptoms. It doesn't make sense. There's a problem with crime in the park. Watching [people] isn't going to fix it. You have to go down to the source of the issue. It would take a lot more money, and it would take a lot more work.

In a similar vein, Vanessa, a white middle class woman was critical of the "quick fix" surveillance systems represented:

> Instead of saying, 'why does our school system not work, why are students going to school and killing each other?' We don't address that. Instead, we say, 'we'll put cameras in every room and it'll be fine.' It never occurs to us, 'wait a minute, there is something fundamentally wrong with the entire system of education.' And why? Because it's too hard. It's too hard. We won't look at it. Instead of saying, 'why are nannies picking up babies and shaking them?' or 'how is it that that someone that can be that abusive could not be screened sufficiently and could end up becoming a nanny?' instead we say, 'no, let's just put a camera in and hope we don't catch our nanny beating our baby.' Instead of looking at the way we run a school, the way we screen nannies, or the way we make a place safe, we just want to slap a camera up and assume that's going to fix everything.

Park visitors' comments regarding the turn to video surveillance as a quick fix also resonate with "technological engineering." Technological engineering aims to solve social problems by using technology, whereas social engineering seeks to invent social, legal, moral, organizational, educational methods to change people's behavior and redirect their activities along ways that are more rational, acceptable and beneficial to the society. Technological solutions might be expensive to develop, but social institutions are attracted to them because they are simpler and their success can be achieved in a relatively easy way. In contrast to "social engineering," which can be complex and frustrating, technological engineering offers "crisp and beautiful" solutions. (Weinberg 1966: 2003, 109, 110).

In terms of video surveillance systems and the creation of the illusion of solution to urban crime, these perspectives on part of some park visitors—if not all— resonate with Ellin's critique of preventive strategies in public places. These strategies provide certain people with a limited sense of security, but do not always diminish actual danger. To the contrary, they contribute to accentuating a more general sense of fear by increasing paranoia and distrust (42). In this sense, the turn to surveillance has succeeded in offering "a Band Aid solution to the ills plaguing the modern city," Ellin maintains (44).

In a similar vein, Roy Coleman (2007) directs our attention to the targeting of persons, behaviors and activities who disrupt urban renewal and entrepreneurialism in the cities. Powerful local agencies implement a set of strategies to reclaim city streets and transform them into risk-free experiences oriented towards consumption and tourism, Coleman notes. Within this framework, surveillance in the city can be seen as an entrepreneurial practice geared to the monitoring of city street space and its potential disruption. "This spatial ordering strategy impinges on the right to decide who walks through a city's streets, and promotes 'safety' for leisured classes…deriding beggars, Goths, skaters as unsightly and unwanted," Coleman contends (237). In this mix of undesirables are also the homeless, the poor, street traders and youth cultures who are disdained as visually unpleasing to the city and aligned with definitions of risk, crime and harm:

> Surveillance in the city…is tied to a strategy of representation and illumination of urban phenomena as signifying 'normal' city life…The rough sleepers, working homeless, street traders, impromptu youth thrill-seekers and those who rely on the 'bargain basement' economy are at risk of being defined negatively (or defined out) of entrepreneurial space (239, 240).

Video Surveillance by Private Entities

So far I have discussed the use of video surveillance in public settings by law enforcement and for crime prevention purposes. However, video surveillance systems are undertaken not only by law enforcement but also by partnership programs between law enforcement and private entities. For example, corporations and/or Business Improvement Districts (BIDs) provide local police departments, which are always cash- strapped, with financial support to purchase surveillance systems, asserting that their primary concern is community safety and well-being.

However, it must be noted that privately-financed surveillance systems are placed in locations where corporations and/or BIDs have interests to protect, and that surveillance cameras are better protectors of property than they are of people. In this light, it can be argued that surveillance systems deployed by private/public partnerships are aligned with corporate not public interests. For example, the surveillance program in downtown Baltimore was initiated by the Business Improvement District, which was concerned with the impact that vandalism and prostitution was having on business in the area. Prompted by the BID, the Baltimore police deployed a large-scale surveillance system with 64 cameras. As noted in the General Accounting Office report on video surveillance, the purpose of the surveillance program was to deter crime and enhance public safety (GAO Report 03-748 2003, 35). However, the location of cameras in Market Center, a retail corridor, made it clear that it was geared primarily towards private interests (Van Sickler 1999, A12).

Similarly, the surveillance system in downtown Minneapolis epitomizes the influence of commercial forces behind several public safety initiatives. In 2004, the Minneapolis City Council approved a gift from the retail giant Target Corporation for at least 30 surveillance cameras to be used by the police department to curb “nuisance crimes.” However, the ten-block area the cameras were placed in is also home to Target’s headquarters and two of its department stores. In a press statement, Target Corporation claimed the gift to the police would help “enhance the safety and vibrancy of downtown Minneapolis for those who live, work, and visit here,” and that the cameras were part of the company’s “longstanding commitment to giving back to the communities in which we do business” (Clements 2004).

Aside from Business Improvement Districts or corporations that seek to create “safe zones” to further their business interests, security companies also cooperate with law enforcement through donations of surveillance equipment as part of their marketing and sales efforts. In Ybor City, for example, the integration of commercial face-scanning and recognition software into the existing video surveillance system in 2001 was the result of cooperation between the police and Identix (formerly Visionics), a leading biometrics company that supplied the software for a free, one-year test (Kinsler 2001). However, after two years of testing with zero positive identifications and zero arrests, the police department eliminated the face recognition software. The 36 cameras that were part of the original surveillance system remain operational (Krause 2003, 1, Dennis 2003, 1).

As one of the most aggressive promoters of biometric technologies and a ubiquitous private contractor, Identix continues to offer its facial recognition system to federal agencies and law enforcement. In 2002, Identix capitalized on a warning of a potential terrorist attack on the Statue of Liberty by immediately supplying facial recognition cameras to the National Park Service, who used them to scan the faces of visitors and compared their pictures with a database of terror suspects (Kilgannon 2002). As one of the officers I interviewed noted, security companies play a significant role in pushing surveillance technology:

> In general they are there to make a dollar. I don't really think they're there to protect anybody. So therefore they sell people the most expensive equipment or whatever they can to get the best profit margin.

Often pressed by private businesses to reassure consumer-citizens, local police departments install surveillance cameras in public spaces where there is little or no actual crime to cut. In the words of Davis (1992), this "search for bourgeois security" is one of the driving forces behind the hardening of public spaces (167). Private businesses exert increasing pressure on local governments and police departments to do something about crime, which is one of the factors resulting in the commercialization of crime control. Visible in several video surveillance and other preventive schemes in urban centers is the new security consciousness "reinforced by the incentives and advice of insurance firms, building societies, tourist guides, and local police" (Garland 2001, 161).

Against the backdrop of these findings and review of literature on social control and crime control, I argue that video surveillance is the product of social institutions' concerns with containment of threats and management of risks and the targeting of resources towards effective control of spaces and of the people within them.

Based on the assumption that crime can be prevented through environmental engineering, the crime control establishment (law enforcement, security industry, citizen-police partnerships, etc.) seeks to harden public spaces by means of preventive measures, prominently surveillance technology. Here the objective is to discourage criminals or would-be offenders from using a given public space or committing violations in that space.

In the generation and intensification of video surveillance, urban planners and developers also play a role. Concerned with regenerating downtown areas or rendering retail environments secure in order to attract businesses and customers, these private entities, often times in collaboration with local law enforcement, deploy surveillance systems and extend cameras into new public settings.

As I have shown earlier, deployment of video surveillance has further increased after September 11, with the aim of preventing future terrorist attacks. Law enforcement officials and federal agencies are especially turning to the integration of face recognition software into video surveillance systems in order to identify terrorists (those who are known and whose images are in databases) in certain places such as airports and landmark locations in major cities. They are also increasing the number of cameras in existing surveillance systems or installing new systems in new places. Although these developments have caused concern on the part of privacy advocates and civil libertarians, law enforcement officials frame the use of video surveillance as an anti-terrorism measure and as part of homeland security efforts, and argue that if people "don't have anything to hide" or are "not doing anything wrong," then they should not be worried about surveillance and its possible implications on privacy. These constructions regarding privacy are explored in Chapter 4.

Notes

[1] See Burge 2004, Mashberg 2004, Grunwald 1996, Cooper 1997, Spielman 2004, Ravo 1998, Scatarella 1993, Garrison 2004, Wall 2004, Hsu 2002, Kinzer 2004, Roe 2008, Savage 2007, Culotta 2009.

[2] Schlosberg Mark and Nicole Ozer (2007) "Under the Watchful Eye: The Proliferation of Video Surveillance Systems in California," American Civil Liberties Union http://www.aclunc.org/docs/criminal_justice/police_practices/under_the_watchful_eye_the_proliferation_of_video_surveillance_systems_in_california.pdf

[3] In addition to these terrestrial surveillance systems, the DHS is also considering to expand the use of spy satellites to enhance border security, secure critical infrastructure, and aid federal and local law enforcement agencies. Traditionally, spy satellites were used to track tank movements during the Cold War by a handful federal civilian agencies for scientific and environmental study. Under the new program, both the DHS and law enforcement officials will have access to real-time, high-resolution imagery and data , which the civil liberties activists criticize as "monitoring from space" leading to an intrusive, omnipresent and invisible network of surveillance. For a detailed discussion, see Block 2007.

[4] Full document of this legislation is available at http://www.epic.org/privacy/surveillance/revised_ regs.html

[5] "DC police set to monitor 5,000 cameras," *The Washington Times*, April 9, 2008, http://washingtontimes.com/news/2008/apr/09/dc-police-set-to-monitor-5000-cameras

[6] Also see Yesil 2006.

[7] Most recent maps of surveillance cameras in New York are available at iSee, a web-based application. iSee charts the locations of cameras and offers users routes that avoid these cameras, "paths of least surveillance, allowing them to walk around their cities without fear of being 'caught on tape' by unregulated security monitors." For more information and maps of surveillance cameras in NYC, visit http://www.appliedautonomy.com/isee.html.

[8] New York Civil Liberties Union (2006) "Who's Watching?: Video Camera Surveillance in New York City and the Need for Public Oversight," http://www.nyclu.org/pdfs/surveillance_cams_report_121306.pdf.

[9] In December 2007, New York City Department of Parks and Recreation started a $16 million renovation project. As a result, the central fountain and some other areas in the park are currently closed For more information, see http://www.nycgovparks.org/sub_your_park/washington_sq_park /reconstruction.php.

[10] Names of all the participants have been changed to pseudonyms.

[11] In his analysis of the pervasive sense of insecurity in Los Angeles, Steven Flusty (1997) notes that all these techniques and strategies of defensive urbanism such as gating, policing and surveillance systems are responses to "uncertainties of a fragmented and dynamic urban milieu" (57). Susan Christopherson (1994) also explains that the social disintegration and increasing economic inequality of the 1980s have made the contemporary city more dangerous. In response, urban designers have emphasized security as a design element and have focused on the control and regulation of human behavior through technology (411).

[12] For a detailed discussion, see Nicholas Fyfe and Jon Bannister's (1998) investigation of video surveillance systems (along with the private policing of office and shopping spaces, and the imposition of nighttime curfews in city-center streets) as a response to anxieties about crime and declining consumer and business confidence in city centers.

CHAPTER 3

Reading, Writing and Surveillance

Video surveillance is fast becoming a part of daily life in American schools. Generally fuelled by concerns over safety, the growing trend of school surveillance has placed school entrances, doors, parking lots, hallways, cafeterias, and even buses under an "extra set of eyes" to prevent violent behavior, maintain discipline, and protect school property.

But are video surveillance systems in schools really successful in achieving deterrence and prevention as law enforcement and school administrators claim? What are the main reasons behind their increasing deployment as a safety and discipline tool? What, if any, are their unintended consequences?

In this chapter, I address these and other questions through a series of in-depth interviews with the New York City Department of Education officials and school administrators in two New York City public schools, as well as students. Further, through interviews with students, I uncover the meanings students attach to video surveillance, and probe how they think and talk about being watched by cameras (Students' conceptualizations of privacy are discussed separately in Chapter 4.)

The Generation and Intensification of the Techno-Security Apparatus in Schools

The use of surveillance cameras and other "safety tools" in New York City public schools is not a new phenomenon. For at least three decades, the city public school system has been tackling the problem of "school safety," a term that politicians and bureaucrats prefer to use instead of the more negative "school violence." The umbrella term of school safety refers to criminal and non-criminal acts committed by students in schools, and it includes major crimes (murder, rape, grand larceny, arson), other crimes (misdemeanor assault, criminal mischief, possession or sale of a controlled substance, possession of marijuana, weapons possession, petit larceny) and non-criminal incidents (disorderly conduct, harassment, loitering, sex offenses, possession of dangerous instruments, and trespassing) (New York City Department of Education 2005). In dealing with these problems, the primary response of the New York City public school system, together with law enforcement, has been to develop a "techno-security apparatus" involving the deployment of police officers and the use of technological devices, such as metal detectors, scanners, ID card systems and surveillance cameras (Devine 1996, 76).

The Division of School Safety, the entity responsible for all safety initiatives, was founded in 1969, as a response to widespread disturbances that occurred during decentralization disputes and teachers' strikes. Over the years, the Division saw a vast expansion in terms of its budget, its reach and the wide array of security measures it uses. For example, the modest body of 200 security officers deployed in troubled high schools as "peace guards" in 1969 had grown considerably to 1,250 in 1980. The following year, the security force consisted of 1,705 members and its coverage spread to junior high schools. By 1994, the number of the Division's uniformed officers had reached a massive 3,200 and its budget $73 million (Van Gelder 1994). Following recent deployments as of 2006, the number of security officers in NYC public schools reached 4,625, making it larger than the entire police force in Boston, Washington D.C., Las Vegas, Detroit Baltimore, Dallas or San Francisco (New York Civil Liberties Union 2007, 10).

The history of the Division of Safety is marked by reorganization efforts, some of them controversial. In 1996, an investigatory commission appointed by Mayor Rudy Giuliani concluded that the Division was poorly managed and failed to maintain security in the schools. The commission suggested that the NYPD should step in and play a greater role in ensuring school safety. In 1998, acting on the commission's recommendation, Mayor Guiliani announced that responsibility for school security, including the training, recruiting, and managing of school safety personnel, would be handed over to the NYPD (Mitchell 1993, New York Civil Liberties Union 2007, 9). The decision to transfer control over school safety to the NYPD worried many families, educators and community leaders, who objected that the plan would create a prison-like environment in schools and would particularly strain the relations between the police and children of color (New York Civil Liberties Union, 8).

Another important step was the reorganization of the Division as the Office of School Safety and Planning. In September 2002, Mayor Michael Bloomberg said their objective in creating the OSSP was to "promote order, improve safety and thus create an environment conducive to learning in the city's public schools" (New York City Department of Education 2003*)*.

In addition to these changes, another important development is the creation of the Impact Schools Initiative. Introduced in January 2004, Impact Schools is a joint effort of the NYPD, Department of Education and the Mayor's Office. It originally targeted 12 schools with high levels of reported crime, however since its creation 26 others schools have been targeted at various times, and the Department of Education intends to address all "problem schools" through this program. In addition to School Safety Agents (see below) already assigned to these schools, the Initiative dedicated an additional task force of at least 200 uniformed police officers and supervisors. Unlike the regular School Safety Agents, these officers are armed with guns (New York Civil Liberties Union, 9). Impact Schools Initiative has been criticized by civil liberties groups as yet another example of over-policing of city schools because it doubles the number of police officers permanently assigned to targeted schools; institutes a zero-tolerance policy for transgressions; and expedites the removal of students via suspension procedures.

The NYPD officers posted to schools are called School Safety Agents (SSA), and they are generally responsible for monitoring lunchrooms, hallways, parking lots, entrance and exits. SSA's are assisted by Deans and/or Assistant Principals who are responsible for disciplinary work in the school, but they have a chain of command independent of the school principal and they report directly to the OSSP. For all practical purposes SSA's are police officers, and their beat is the school. They wear NYPD uniforms and have badges, maintain contact via walkie-talkies, do not carry guns but can make arrests (Devine 1996, 77). Most high schools have between ten and twenty SSA's and one to three police officers permanently assigned to the school. Middle schools also have several safety agents and some have permanent police presence as well (NESRI—National Economic and Social Rights Initiative 2007, 35).

Aside from the police presence, another component of the techno-security apparatus in New York City schools is the metal detectors, first installed in 1981 in a Brooklyn high school as part of a pilot program to search for weapons. However, because of student riots protesting their use, metal detector systems were quickly dismantled. In 1989, the Division gave metal detectors another trial run, this time in five high schools. By 1992 metal detectors were firmly in place in 19 high schools and two middle schools, and eventually spread to 41 schools in 1993 (Barnabel 1993). By 2006, according to city reports, 21 percent of middle schools and high schools, 82 public schools in total, were scanning students using permanent metal detectors on a daily basis. A New York Civil Liberties Union (2007) investigation revealed that students on even more campuses than these 82 – at least 93,411 students attending at least 88 schools – must pass through permanent metal detectors to enter their school buildings each day. Aside from these permanent detectors at school entrances, NYPD also deploys "roving" detectors or scanners at any given school unannounced. They have been deployed since 2006, as part of Mayor Bloomberg's new safety initiative, subjecting all middle school and high school students to scanners, designed to catch them by surprise and to reduce the number of weapons in the school (NESRI, 10).

In addition to police presence and metal detectors, New York City school system has also turned to surveillance cameras as part of the larger security apparatus it has been developing and deploying in schools. According to Richard Glover, the Executive Director of the Office of School Safety and Planning in the New York City Department of Education, surveillance cameras were first used in 1985 or 1986 (there is still no certainty as to the exact date) at the South Shore High School in Brooklyn as part of an experiment conducted by the School Facilities Department. South Shore was picked at random, and the fifty cameras placed in the school were financed by "a politician or a councilman who made available his personal funds for this [experiment]." Although the Division of School Safety was initially critical of this "operation" for its randomness both in the selection of the school and the placement of cameras, it ultimately "let the School Facilities handle [it] and expand cameras to other schools" (author's interview).

According to another Department of Education official working in the Division of School Facilities, the "eye in the sky" has been in use since late 1980s, particularly in large and troubled high schools. However, surveillance cameras have recently spread from the more notorious high schools to others regardless of student population or crime level, as well as to middle schools. In 2002, Schools Chancellor Joel Klein revealed a comprehensive plan that included, among other components, the deployment of more School Safety Agents and the use of more surveillance cameras to address safety and discipline problems. Klein said that eleven of the city's most troubled high schools would get cameras, noting that they have "a positive effect" on school safety. This would increase the number of high schools with cameras to about 40 out of a total of 200 (Median 2002, Ginsberg 2002). NYPD Commissioner Raymond Kelly also noted that the "increase in School Safety Agents combined with the installation of closed circuit television cameras in select schools will enhance the Police Department's ability to make New York City schools safer" (New York City Department of Education 2003). As of late 2004, there were cameras in 150 of the 1,000 public schools in NYC. But the numbers are likely to increase. In 2003, New York City councilman Peter Vallone led a drive to appropriate $1million for cameras in three notorious high schools, and noted that ubiquitous video surveillance "is definitely the movement we are headed to" (Dillon 2003).

In November 2004, the City Council passed a bill to install more surveillance cameras in schools. In addition to the $120 million set aside to put cameras in 350 schools, the Council hopes to expand its plan to every school. Councilman Peter Vallone described the bill as a "big first step towards my goal of putting cameras in every school in the city." A Department of Education spokesman said the school system is making good progress in safety by installing cameras (Bennett 2004).

The Office of School Safety and Planning also promised coordinated and effective use of surveillance cameras across the city, and announced plans to procure more technologically advanced surveillance systems, such as the fully digital and networked system employed in Washington, D.C. schools. The main reason for pushing these new systems has to do with response time in case of tragic events, such as the Columbine shootings. The Columbine High School had surveillance cameras, but they were unable to prevent or stop the shootings, which the security companies have capitalized on to demonstrate the need for digital and real-time surveillance (and of course to increase their profits). These systems connect real-time to the local police station or the security company's headquarters via the web, so in case of an incident the police can be alerted and respond in a timely manner—at least theoretically. In some applications, school principals or superintendents can gain remote access to web pages that display live footage from the school or the system can feed images to emergency operators and to wireless laptop computers of first responders or to police cruisers (author's interview).

The conversion from analog to digital camera and recording systems, and the citywide networking was carried out in April 2007. The $120 million system, called the Internet Protocol Digital Video Surveillance (IPDVS), includes cameras linked by a network to a main server in each school. Video is watched live by SSA's from a monitoring console; it can also be viewed live and archived remotely at Department of Education headquarters. According to Department of Education, as of April 2007, IPDVS was installed in 60 buildings and 163 schools (because some buildings are home to more than one school) (Winston 2007).

According to School Construction Authority (SCA), which oversees all public school construction, there are about six to 10 cameras in schools smaller than 50,000 square feet; while there can be up to 96 cameras in schools larger than 350,000 square feet, such as large high schools. IPDVS cameras are now mandated for every new SCA project, and Councilman Vallone says another 59 schools are currently being equipped with cameras (Winston 2007). By the end of 2008, another 6,000 IPDVS cameras will be installed at more than 300 middle and high schools. (Winston 2008).

Video Surveillance as Preventive Measure

In his statement about the OSSP's school safety plan, Chancellor Joel Klein noted that surveillance cameras would be of help because "students don't do anything wrong when they know there's monitoring going on" (Ginsberg 2002). The idea that surveillance cameras "prevent people from doing stupid things" is one of the predominant themes to emerge from the Department of Education rhetoric. Bureaucrats point out that surveillance cameras in schools perform a variety of positive functions, from “eliminating loitering and graffiti” to “preventing horrific events like shootings” to “keeping children in line.” The major concern here is prevention couched in concern for safety. As one Department of Education official responsible for school facilities and camera deployment noted,

> If we did nothing, you wouldn’t have peace of mind. You wouldn’t have faith in your government or your educational system to provide safety. What we’re doing is taking the extra measures thinking something can happen. We say, ‘Let’s try to prevent it.’ It’s like a military person preparing for an attack, putting his troops in the right places. [School] security is the same thing. Prevention is a big factor.

To understand why Department of Education bureaucrats and (some) school administrators think of cameras as a preventive measure, we must investigate the incorporation of security technologies into the larger social control practices in schools.

From the 1980s onwards, schools have directed attention to prevention of risks and manipulation of environmental factors in order to maintain student discipline, prevent crime, and protect property. The entrepreneurial impulse concerning the schools has been towards a “massive investment in hardware and preventive technology: video surveillance, ultrasonic detectors, hotlines to the police, redesigning buildings into clusters of manageable of space” (Cohen 1983, 80). Digital or analog camera systems, ID cards, biometrics, electronic gates, two-way radios, transparent lockers and book bags are some of the most common surveillance devices used at schools today. Such integration of law enforcement functions into the everyday life at schools subsequently creates a culture of control supplanting other social or educational missions as well as accruing more power to law enforcement personnel over school operations, especially those concerning student discipline and risk management (Monahan 2006, 110, 113).

These developments concerning the turn to preventive surveillance are consequences of a new movement in crime control, one that relies on preventing risks rather than rehabilitating the individual offender. As I have discussed in detail in the preceding chapter, this movement, which emerged in the 1970s as a response to the failure of previous crime control models, has defined crime not as an individual deviance but as a set of preventable risks, and as a result has directed attention to the creation of defensible spaces, hardening of potential targets and investment in hardware and preventive technologies, most prominently surveillance technologies (Cohen 146-148, O'Malley 1996, 190).

Seen in this light, it is no coincidence that from the 1970s onwards, the Division of School Safety expanded vastly, and came to rely on the techno-security apparatus to resolve violence and discipline issues. It would be simplistic to examine the deployment of surveillance cameras in schools as merely a technological issue. New York City public school system did not introduce metal detectors or surveillance cameras simply because these technological devices were finally available on the market or were deemed more effective than their predecessors. What galvanized the rise and spread of the techno-security apparatus in schools did not have to do with technology on its own, but with the mindset that regarded technology as a remedy to social problems, and more significantly with the crime control initiatives that increasingly came to rely on technology to manage dangers and minimize risks. Therefore, the deployment of video surveillance in schools is not merely a technological development, but rather a social, political process in affinity with trends in the field of crime control. Of importance in this social, political process is the perception of video surveillance as a silver bullet to public safety issues. Alarmed by the rising fear of crime in urban spaces (which can be unsubstantiated) and the collapsing sense of public safety, policymakers generally usher in video surveillance as a quick fix.

Along these lines, high-level bureaucrats in the New York City public school system frame surveillance cameras as a remedy to school safety issues, and tend to deflect attention away from significant causes of safety and discipline problems such as those stemming from urban poverty, and instead point the finger at student behavior. In mystifying the relationship between school safety and student behavior, these bureaucrats portray surveillance cameras as the ultimate remedy.

The deployment of surveillance systems in schools is also fuelled by politicians', bureaucrats' and school administrators' efforts to quell fear of crime and violence in schools, especially on the part of parents. The institutionalization of fear of crime as a prominent cultural theme over the last thirty years has set the emotional tone for public discourse and policies about crime and punishment. Among significant side effects of this development are the decreasing public confidence in the ability of the criminal justice system, demands for stronger measures of punishment and protection, and the belief on the part of a large majority of the public that crime rates are getting worse (regardless of the actual patterns) (Garland 2001, 152-54).

In response to the fear of crime in schools, especially after the Columbine shootings, schools have been turning to video surveillance as a preventive measure, and more importantly as part of their public relations efforts. Ironically, those who pitch cameras as safety tools rarely mention the fact that Columbine High School had surveillance cameras at the time of the shootings only to capture the tragic events on tape, not prevent them from happening in the first place.

To explore what specific purposes video surveillance serves in schools and to investigate its day-to-day operations, in the following pages I present my findings from interviews conducted with school administrators (assistant principals and/or deans) in two New York City public schools. For the sake of anonymity, I refer to these schools by the pseudonyms of Lincoln Middle School and Jefferson High School. The names of administrators and students who participated in this study have also been changed.

Lincoln Middle School

Lincoln Middle School is located in the eastern section of New York City in a neighborhood that is home to African-American, Hispanic and Southeast Asian populations. It is one of the biggest middle schools in the city with 2,700 students enrolled in grades six through eight. The student population, described as "tough" by the administrators, is 44% Southeast Asian, 21% African-American, 30% Hispanic and 3% white. Lincoln Middle School consists of two buildings connected to each other and two trailers in the backyard, which are used as classrooms.

I visited Lincoln Middle School for the first time in February 2003. When I arrived for my meeting with the principal, it was around 10 a.m., and the students were already in class, which made the entrance area particularly quiet. My first impression of Lincoln was that it did not feel particularly welcoming. I had to push open a very heavy steel door only to be greeted with a stern police officer who was sitting behind a console, known as the "security desk." As I stepped in, she looked up and gave me a "What are you doing here?" look. I told her I was there to see Ms. Suarez, the principal. After showing my ID and signing in, I idled for a few minutes taking off my coat and such, so I could look around. I noticed two things: On the security desk, there was a large monitor, which was split into about a dozen screens displaying footage from surveillance cameras. On one screen, I caught a glimpse of students wandering in a hallway. Another screen showed an empty staircase. On another screen, there was simply static. I also saw a big sign on the wall, which said in bold, capital letters, "No hats, no baseball caps, no hoods, no walkman, no cell phones, no radios, no tank tops, no shorts." I started walking down the long hallway trying to take in the atmosphere of the school. There was no doubt that Lincoln Middle School cared about safety and discipline. It had rules. It had security officers. And it had surveillance cameras. So what were the specific reasons behind these safety and discipline measures, especially the cameras? Why did Lincoln administrators think they needed them? What problems did they seek to solve? What were students' constructions of the cameras? And how did these constructions come into being? These were some of the questions I hoped to answer in my research in Lincoln Middle School.

During the course of seven visits, I immersed myself in the everyday life of Lincoln. My research aimed to understand the use and outcomes of surveillance cameras, not to determine whether Lincoln was "dangerous" or whether the students were "violent." I focused on the safety and security culture of the school, and tried to explore the administrators' and students' constructions of video surveillance against this background. I interviewed two deans who are in charge of school safety and discipline, and six students. I roamed the hallways trying to locate surveillance cameras, hung out in the cafeteria during lunch hour to observe student behavior, and even spent time in the "detention center" where students who cause major discipline problems are placed for the day.

Video Surveillance at Lincoln Middle School

According to the two deans I interviewed, Mr. Miller and Mr. Thompson, Lincoln is not particularly a "dangerous" school. Mr. Miller said there are no stabbings, shootings, or gang problems at Lincoln — things that in his judgment define a school as dangerous or violent. But as he further discussed safety and discipline issues, Mr. Miller spoke of some incidents that happened at the beginning of the 2002-03 academic year, whereby a student assaulted a teacher, and some students extorted each other for money. Faced with such "tremendous problems," he said, he and Mr. Thompson brought a task force to the school to solve discipline and safety issues. Mr. Thompson, the other dean who is also the UFT representative at Lincoln, explained that the task force, which consisted of UFT officials, the district superintendent and the police

> had several meetings every two or three weeks; got the police involved; came up with things to make it better. We froze registration so no more students would be enrolled, 'cause new people moving to the neighborhood and their kids coming to this school. So we shut down registration. We added surveillance cameras, security agents. And got more radios, walkie-talkies and gave them to people working at the school to secure the school.

As a result, according to Mr. Thompson, the school administration has been able to establish and maintain a sense of normalcy in the school.

As I learned from Mr. Miller and Mr. Thompson, there are sixteen surveillance cameras located in Lincoln Middle School, in the hallways and staircases. Based on my observations, I identified fourteen of them as first-generation cameras, which have no pan, tilt or zoom functions. The other two, which were added at the beginning of the 2002-03 academic year, are second-generation cameras with pan, tilt and zoom functions. One of the fourteen first-generation cameras is used to monitor the yard, but since it is fixed in position and cannot tilt or pan, it does not cover the whole yard. This means that the area around trailers is not under surveillance. According to Mr. Miller and Mr. Thompson, students who know about this usually go behind the trailers when they cut classes or smoke. There are five security officers at Lincoln, and they patrol the hallways and the cafeteria on a continuous basis, and check the yard on occasion. One officer is assigned to the security desk by the entrance, and screens the camera footage on the monitors.

Deployment of surveillance cameras and SSA's at Lincoln Middle School

Number of surveillance cameras	16
Location of surveillance cameras	Hallways, staircases, yard
Is surveillance footage recorded on tape?	No
Who is monitoring the surveillance footage?	SSAs assigned to the security desk by the entrance
Total number of SSA's	5

In separate interviews, I asked Mr. Miller and Mr. Thompson what purpose the video surveillance system served. They said it was mainly for identifying the students who pull the fire alarms, cut classes or hang out in the hallways. Both Mr. Miller and Mr. Thompson told me that they do not think the surveillance system deters the students or prevents undesirable behaviors. In contrast to bureaucrats and politicians who claim that surveillance cameras establish and maintain discipline by "turning students into little angels because they know they are being watched," these deans presented a different picture regarding video surveillance and its preventive capabilities. According to Mr. Thompson,

> [Students] don't [become little angels] here. After a while they are so acclimated to [cameras'] presence that they don't care. They do what they do. They are not thinking of the cameras. They do whatever they do irrespective of the cameras.

Mr. Miller echoed:

> We still have fights. Kids are gonna be kids. If they feel like getting into a fight they are gonna get into a fight. I don't think [cameras] make them behave better. When they cut

> classes, they will go to the staircase where there are no cameras. So once they leave the hallway, the camera doesn't know.

In Lincoln Middle School, video surveillance, according to these deans' accounts, helps to catch students who pull fire alarms or leave the building without permission, and it can be effective in identifying "perpetrators" who start fights or steal money from teachers. These are the *corollary benefits* of video surveillance, that is video surveillance can help to identify and/or track a student or a group of students *after* they commit a violation, but does not necessarily deter them. What are the insights these deans have to offer into this phenomenon? They say, first and foremost, students know where the cameras are located, and if they are intent on doing something they simply go to an area that is not surveilled. As Mr. Miller explains,

> Some of the kids are so smart they know that 'Wow, it's a camera there next to that fire alarm. I'm not going to pull that alarm. But wow there isn't a camera over here on that floor and it's a fire alarm right there so let me just run and pull that one.' And they know they'll never get caught.

Further, Mr. Miller and Mr. Thompson note that the failure of the surveillance system in producing changes on student behavior is also the result of the problem of human observers. They say surveillance cameras on their own achieve nothing. Regardless of its technical features (number of cameras or their zoom, pan, tilt and focus functions, etc) the crucial component of the surveillance system is the human observer who watches the monitors, attentively scans the surveillance footage and does something about what s/he sees. Mr. Thompson's comments clarify this point regarding the failure of a system that is rich in terms of technological resources but poor in personnel:

> Last year when we had three deans, [one of us would look at the cameras] and say "Hey there's somebody up there on that floor. Go up on this floor and check that out." So we were like hawks. But now because of budget cuts, they had to cut down personnel; and they even cut down school safety people. And now there's nobody to watch the monitors.

When I mentioned the SSA at the security desk who is watching the surveillance footage—at least in theory, he shook his head and says, "Not always, not carefully." Despite these "shortcomings," both Mr. Miller and Mr. Thompson seemed to be in favor of the surveillance system. When I asked them why, to learn how they developed this construction, they said that parents who are worried about their children's safety, and the teachers who sometimes find themselves as the target of violent behavior consider video surveillance a tangible response to the problem of school safety.

Both deans contended that using surveillance cameras is a way of showing to parents and teachers that the school administration is "doing something about safety." Mr. Miller added, "You just don't want to be on the front page of the *Daily News* or the *New York Post* because some students went wacko like they did in that school in the Bronx and now they have the army down there."

This remark suggests that school administrators are worried about violent incidents not just because they threaten the well being of students, teachers and staff, but they also create bad publicity for the school. School administrators are anxious not to have their school labeled as a dangerous or a violent one in the public eye, because then the school becomes the focus of too much attention from the Department of Education and the NYPD, as well as the media.

In his analysis of risk management and social control in schools, Torin Monahan (2006) directs attention to the role of media reports in the generation of culture of control in schools. Monahan argues that despite the statistics which show a steady decrease in school violence, media portrayals of school violence generates a culture of fear casting students as victims or criminals who need to be protected or controlled by law enforcement. Media reports about the public's heightened concerns over school safety and the well-being of our "children," serve to justify existence of surveillance systems and law enforcement functions in schools. Media reports transform idiosyncratic events into universal threats, produce fears about school safety, call for more surveillance and police presence in schools and thus play a complicit role in this control regime (116-120).

Going back to administrators framing of school safety measures both in positive and negative terms, it is important to note that they reflect on video surveillance as a good way of demonstrating their safety efforts, but they add that too much of it is not a good thing.

These comments resonate with David Lyon's (1994, 2003, 2007) discussion of the paradoxical nature and experience of surveillance systems. Lyon argues that surveillance exists for a host of reasons that can be located on a continuum from care to control. Surveillance is used not only to keep track of personal lives, but also to enable individuals to participate in social and economic life, protecting and enhancing their life chances. Because it has two faces, Lyon notes, surveillance is perceived and experienced ambivalently in terms of both positive and negative consequences, and it is not uncommon to see the costs of surveillance being overshadowed by its benefits. In light of Lyon's discussion, we can make sense of how the administrators in Lincoln Middle School construct video surveillance in a paradoxical fashion, and regard it as an embodiment of both care and control.

Students' Constructions of Video Surveillance

From the interviews I had with students in Lincoln Middle School, what emerged was a generally positive perception of video surveillance in terms of the reasons behind its deployment. Students considered the use of surveillance cameras along with the presence of police officers as an indication of the school administration's efforts to make Lincoln a safe place. Comments such as "they say cameras are there for our safety," "they put cameras to keep the school safe" or "cameras protect us" transpired repeatedly in the interviews. How do these constructions that are accepting of surveillance come into being? What dynamics shape students' thinking about surveillance cameras?

In general, students viewed the surveillance system as well as the presence of police officers in a positive light because they believed these measures made their school a better place by helping to catch students who pull fire alarms or by protecting them from bullies, gang members or intruders. John, an 8th grade student said, "They say it keeps the school safe. Like from gang members coming into school."

Marcy, a 6th grade student spoke of the feeling of safety she gets from the surveillance system: "Like when there's a bully trying to hit you, you go like, 'You can't hit me because there's cameras and there's also guards and police; and security and the principal could come and they could suspend you.' And they stay away from you." Janet, an 8th grade student offered the following explanation:

> They say it's for our safety and they say they want us to have a better learning environment. They say they have cameras so that whoever is stopping you from learning or that is causing all the trouble can get kicked out of the school. So that it will be more peaceful in the classroom. They say it's for our safety and they want us to learn more and to grow up to be nice, intelligent young women and men, as they always say.

Janet's comments about the benefits of video surveillance can help us understand how students' constructions come into being, especially when examined against the background of what administrators tell students about the safety initiatives they deploy.

When I asked students what they thought about surveillance cameras, they generally framed their responses around the administrators' or teachers' discourse. They said, for example, "*they say* cameras are there for our safety" or "*they say* cameras help the security guards do their job," etc.

It can be argued that these students did not reflect on surveillance until I asked them about it, so they simply reiterated what others had to say. But during in-depth interviews, students elaborated and brought to surface their own constructions, especially during moments of ambivalence. For example, they discussed in detail the ineffectiveness of the surveillance system, and criticized administrators and security officers. Marcy said human observers often times did not pay any attention to the surveillance footage and thus rendered it useless:

> Sometimes the security guards at the security desk, they are not looking at the cameras. Sometimes they are talking to one another. Things are going on the camera. Yeah, you have cameras but there's nobody watching it. You can't do

> anything with them. What are you gonna do with the cameras even if you are not paying any attention to it?

Janet expressed concern about security officers' behaviors:

> Some security guards are friends with some of the bad kids. And when they catch them on camera, they let them slide. They don't understand that they let you slide they are causing more trouble. Cause the same kids keep doing the same things over and over. And they get away with it.

Meanwhile, John jokingly said security officers' inattentiveness was good for him, since in his words, he is not a "perfect student" and that he gets into trouble sometimes. John was never caught on camera, but he says that his likelihood of apprehension is high because he "picks a fight every now and then." But he is one of those "smart" students who knows how to escape the gaze of the surveillance system:

> Me and my friend, we had a fight one day. And we was like 'Wait there's a camera here, go upstairs.' 'No, no, there is a camera. Let's go there, there's no camera.' So you know where the cameras are, so you move your fight. You go where there are no cameras.

John identifies himself as a potential target of the surveillance system and therefore as someone who needs to escape its gaze in order not to be apprehended. But interestingly he is also appreciative of video surveillance, especially when it comes to the (supposed) protection it offers regarding gang members or intruders. He says, "I don't like cameras cause it can see me, but when you think about it, it's good for the school. I mean it can stop gangs from coming inside. So they are good thing." Here, we can see how video surveillance is experienced in ambivalent terms since it is both about control and care. John, as a student who is a potential target of the surveillance system is nevertheless accepting of it, and commends the school administration for its efforts to make Lincoln a safer and a better place.[1]

This should once again direct our attention to the ambiguous nature of surveillance or its dialectics. Generally the term surveillance conjures up images of repression and control. Yet as Lyon and others show, surveillance is not only about malevolence but also about convenience and care.[2] The garnering of personal data by institutions facilitates entitlement, efficiency, convenience or security. Documentation and recording systems collect our personal information but also make life easier: convenience of credit cards, for example. Yet at the same time, information collected by credit agencies may have a negative impact on one's eligibility for a mortgage. Surveillance is ambiguous then. It seems to enable as well as constrain.

The dialectics of surveillance, that it simultaneously constrains and empowers, is also about the voluntary participation of individuals in surveillance systems. Within the context of the information age and data/electronic surveillance, contemporary surveillance systems are viewed differently from the old Benthamite or Orwellian Panopticons. Through their benefits, these systems enable the individuals to participate in consumer society; it is the source of goods. Individuals voluntarily participate in surveillance programs because they see benefits instead of disadvantages or threats. The convenience of ATMs, telephone and online banking, credit, debit and smart cards make surveillance "predominantly consensual" (Whitaker 1999, 139).

In a similar vein, surveillance is beneficial because it establishes and maintains reputations in a society of strangers. Surveillance methods such as credit cards, driver's licenses, drug tests, lie detector tests, genetic and biochemical recordings enable anonymous strangers to trust and enter into social relationships with one another (Nock 1993, Lyon 2007). Yet it must also be noted that surveillance is differential in its empowering or enabling powers: "The same Panopticon that issues inclusive benefits, punishes by exclusion. The same detailed surveillance that personalizes benefits, targets those to be excluded from benefits" (Whitaker, 142).

Safety and Discipline

During my visits to Lincoln, I spent time hanging out in the hallways and the lunchroom to observe the interactions between administrators and students. What did they say to students for example when they caught them fighting? What did they tell them about safety and discipline rules?

Mr. Miller and Mr. Thompson had earlier told me that they focus on the value of a safe and orderly school in order to explain to students why they should not fight or pull the fire alarms. These are disruptive behaviors taking away time and energy from learning and education, they tell students.

During one of my visits, I had the chance to observe Mr. Thompson, and on one particular occasion I observed him respond to a fight between two female students. When he received a call on his walkie-talkie about the fight, Mr. Thompson rushed upstairs only to find a police officer trying to stop the students from hitting each other. It was during class period so the hallway was empty except for the two other female students standing by and watching the fight. Mr. Thompson did not get involved, but rather waited for the police officer to break up the fight, who I noticed was trying to do so using his elbows not his hands. (Later on, I learned that deans did their best not to get physically engaged with students when trying to break up a fight for fear of being accused of harassment). Of course, in the meantime Mr. Thompson was telling the students to stop—his voice at a rather high decibel. When the fight was finally over after about five minutes, Mr. Thompson and the police officer ushered the students into Mr. Thompson's office. The officer said he didn't know what exactly started the fight and that he happened to stumble upon the girls, and he left. Mr. Thompson asked the students to sit down at a desk, gave them a piece of paper and a pen and said, "Now write your statement about what happened." While they were busy writing, Mr. Thompson called the principal's office and told a staff member that he was bringing two students for disciplinary action. As the students were finishing up, he lectured them on why it was wrong to get into a fight (because it doesn't solve your problems and interferes with your education) and warned them about the consequences (if you don't get a good education, you will end up flipping burgers). It could very well be that Mr. Thompson made those specific remarks in that specific manner because of my presence. But on two other occasions, I observed a teacher and an assistant principal making similar comments to students they caught fist fighting in the hallways.

In light of the link that administrators and teachers establish between safety and learning, it is not surprising then that they also portray the safety measures they deploy in a positive light. As Janet explains, students are told that undesirable behaviors are framed as obstacles to a "safe learning environment."

My objective here is not to assess the validity of these arguments, but rather to direct attention to how they shape students' constructions of safety and surveillance in the school. Administrators tell students that they use video surveillance for their well being, out of concern for their safety and education, and emphasize the care motif. This helps to explain why students like Marcy, Janet and John do not seem to be bothered by the control dimension of video surveillance. This is so primarily because they view video surveillance as a safety tool, which is a construction created and circulated by the administrators (and teachers) in the first place.

Of course, this is not to say that other students who participated in this study have the same constructions of video surveillance. Two students I interviewed, James and Robert expressed indifference towards cameras' control function, and said it did not bother them. But unlike Marcy, Janet and John, they did not construct nor accept video surveillance as a safety tool. As a matter of fact they showed no interest in these matters. They said they did not behave any differently just because the cameras were watching them. For example, James, an eight-grade student, said he sometimes cut classes and hung out in the staircases or in the yard but never thought of changing his behaviors. He said, "I just go about my business. When there is a camera I don't care."

Underlying James's indifference to social control is the conviction that "security guards are not looking at the cameras" and that they "let things slide." But as I learned from James, there is also the thrill of "doing something in front of a camera" and then "running away from [it.]" He said: "You go to the fire alarm, act like you are pulling it. And wave at the cops." Although James never did pull the fire alarm or intentionally got into a fight under the gaze of a camera, he said his friends did, not only for the thrill but also for "a little bit of glory" in the eyes of their peers, to "prove something" or just to hear their friends say, "Wow, you did it! Oh wow, you are so cool."

During my visits to Lincoln, I saw students waving, smiling, and pulling faces at the cameras. As Robert told me "some kids do things straight to the security cameras. They stick their finger straight to the camera. People put their faces in front of the camera," which are not acts worthy of apprehension. According to Robert and James' explanation, some students also see being caught on camera as a milestone in establishing a reputation in the school. Be it for acceptance or their fifteen minutes of fame, they perform for their audience, consisting of their peers, security officers and the principal or assistant principals. (Although students don't get to see the footage on monitors, they watch the performance in the act itself, and thus constitute an audience.)

It can be argued that students' use of surveillance cameras for performative purposes is reflective of broader cultural forces, most prominently the "celebrity factor." Some students intentionally engage in transgression in front of the cameras and transform them into tools of spectacle, rendering them useless in terms of control and prevention. Therefore, surveillance cameras are turned into vehicles through which some students voluntarily establish visibility. These young adolescents, who grow up and live in a culture that valorizes being on camera and being seen by the many, blur the line between surveillance and spectacle. As Robert said, "Some kids like attention, and they are gonna keep on doing it because they think it's funny." James added: "Sometimes you go like you'll be cool if you cut class and the cameras caught you. You be laughing at the cameras when you see them."

Jefferson High School

The other school where research was conducted is the Jefferson High School, located in the eastern part of New York City, in a neighborhood dotted with housing projects. Like most other high schools in the city, Jefferson High has a diverse student body. Of the 2,200 students enrolled in grades nine through twelve, 53% are African-American, 27 % Hispanic, 16% white and 3% Asian, reflecting the ethnic makeup of the neighborhood.

I visited Jefferson High for the first time in March 2003. When I got off the subway and started walking down the block towards the school, it was around 8 a.m. I saw students walking hurriedly trying to make it to class on time—a usual scene, I thought. But what was unusual—at least to me—was the presence of two NYPD patrol cars parked on street corners and four officers monitoring the students coming to the school. I thought something must have happened.

When I arrived at the school, there was a line of about 10 students waiting to enter the building. They were showing ID's and having their backpacks examined by the security officers, similar to the rite at Lincoln Middle School, which I experienced one time when I got there earlier than usual. When it was my turn, one of the two officers told me to step aside and asked me the purpose of my visit. I explained that I had an appointment with Mr. Smith, the assistant principal, and showed my ID and signed in. Since I knew what to expect thanks to my experience at Lincoln, this time I was not surprised that entry into a public school in New York City meant going through a security check, both for the students and the visitors, but not administrators, teachers or staff. Also predictable was the presence of the monitor at the security desk displaying surveillance footage and that big sign on the wall with the long list of No's on it. What was surprising though was the presence of patrol cars and officers outside the building and on the street. During the course of my next eight visits to Jefferson High, I realized that the time of the day when students were coming to or leaving the school coincided with heavy police presence on surrounding streets which aimed to create a "safety zone" around the school. This was especially spurred by the fear of gang members (both Lincoln students and outsiders) meeting in front of the school. Mr. Smith, the assistant principal, explained that this was part of the citywide school safety initiative especially in high schools to prevent students from idling or congregating on street corners.

At Jefferson High, it is not only the outside of the building but also the inside that is subject to monitoring. Hallways and staircases are under the gaze of SSA's who try to deter students by way of their presence. And these areas are also under video surveillance.

Video Surveillance at Jefferson High School

At Jefferson High, there are 110 first-generation and 16 second-generation cameras watching hallways, staircases and the cafeteria. Surveillance footage from the first-generation cameras is viewed in the control room by two security officers who monitor the streaming video and alert other officers and/or administrators in case of an emergency situation. The footage from the second-generation cameras is viewed at the security desk by one police officer. Overall, there are 19 officers deployed at Jefferson High. In comparison to Lincoln Middle School, Jefferson High has a much larger number of cameras and police officers, which according to school administrators in both schools, is due to the assumption that high school students are "rougher" than middle school students. Mr. Smith also adds that the Jefferson building is quite large with four separate modules, and hallways are not straight but curvilinear creating blind spots and therefore requiring more cameras.

Deployment of surveillance cameras and SSA's at Jefferson High School

Number of surveillance cameras	110 analog (5 broken) and 16 digital
Location of surveillance cameras	Hallways, cafeteria, perimeter of the school
Is surveillance footage recorded on tape?	No
Who is monitoring the surveillance footage?	2 SSAs in the control room and one SSA assigned to the security desk by the entrance

During the course of eight visits, I sought to explore the safety and security initiatives at Jefferson High, particularly the surveillance system. I conducted interviews with students, and administrators who are in charge of school safety and discipline, Mr. Smith, the assistant principal and Mr. Casey, the dean, who is also the United Federation of Teachers representative. I spent time in the hallways and the lunchroom to observe student behavior, and the interactions between students and administrators and security officers. My objective was not to determine whether Jefferson High is a safe or a dangerous school, but to understand why and in what ways it used video surveillance cameras, and to explore administrators' and students' constructions of them.

According to Mr. Smith and Mr. Casey, Jefferson High is not a dangerous school, but an "unruly" and a "disorderly" one. This is so because of the "rough student population" which is exacerbated by the "lack of continuity in administration and disciplinary procedures." Within the last two years, Jefferson High had two different principals, and three different assistant principals in charge of school safety. As Mr. Casey suggested, the lack of cooperation between the principal, assistant principals, deans and security officers also makes the task of school safety and discipline a particularly difficult one.

In response to my inquiry about the reasons behind the deployment of surveillance cameras, both Mr. Smith and Mr. Casey said their objective was to "keep an eye on students" students to prevent them from causing personal injury to one another or to teachers, and to deter them from pulling the fire alarms or cutting classes. However, as they elaborated on their response, it became clear that these administrators did not necessarily think video surveillance achieved these goals. Mr. Smith said surveillance cameras helped them to catch students after they did something wrong, but in general he was quite pessimistic about cameras' preventive capabilities. He said video surveillance is like "putting a band-aid on a cancer that's spreading and there's nothing you can do about it:"

> I mean, let's face it, we still have children who are fighting; we still have children who, once in a while, pull off the alarms. Even when they see the camera, they still do it. And then we go and pick them up and then they get suspended. So they get to go home for two or three days, they sit in their house, playing with their Nintendo. They call their friends, "Listen, I'm in the house, come over here." Hello? It makes it even worse.

In demystifying the hypothesis that video surveillance deters potential wrongdoers, he openly expressed his dismay with high-level officials' claims:

> It's lip service. They go to one of the hotels, the Hilton or whatever, and they have big meetings, all of the teachers go from the UFT, the governor goes, the mayor goes, and everybody is talking about all of the wonderful things they are going to be implementing in our schools, and it's a fantasy. They always want to bring cameras. Nothing has changed. And, I think it has to do with [the fact that] people at the local and federal level that are making all of these decisions that are affecting our schools and our communities, they don't even have an idea of the reality of what's going on. And I say, "Have you ever been in one of the schools

> that we come from?" They have this utopian mentality that everything is wonderful and if you do it this way, it is going to work.

Meanwhile, Mr. Casey argued that video surveillance can be effective if used properly. He said "it doesn't hurt, it's like chicken soup." To clarify how surveillance cameras can be effective (or not) in prevention, Mr. Casey told me about an incident in which he was wrongly accused of harassing a female student. In his account, the incident was triggered by students congregating by the cafeteria, a surveilled area. "If [the camera system] was being used correctly," he said "the officer in the [camera] room would call another officer saying you have a large group of kids by the cafeteria, please go down and disperse them." But according to Mr. Casey, there was no one in the "camera room" to watch the streaming video and dispatch security officers to the cafeteria, which resulted in things "getting out of control:"

> There was a student there who was busy dancing with her walkman on her head as if she were in the disco. I walked over because you're not supposed to have that, you're not supposed to be wearing it, you're supposed to be in class. And I walked over and I wanted to get her attention, I wanted to get the walkman. One thing led to another and she decided she was going to strangle me by my lanyard. And she was… she was yanking and yanking and yanking. Then her friend told her to yell sexual harassment, which she then started yelling. And this went on. So eventually after about 10-15 minutes of her yelling officers finally came. That's 10 or 15 minutes too long. If someone had been watching [the footage] in the camera room, that should have taken a minute or so for a response. A student who was insubordinate, who was assaulting a staff member, who was cutting class…she walked free and I ended up under investigation. I've been cleared, but the bottom line is I never should have been under investigation.

In this account, we find an administrator's frustration with the way surveillance cameras are used. Like the deans and students in Lincoln

Middle School, Mr. Casey directs attention to the significance of the human observers, and reveals that in some cases the surveillance system cannot even monitor safety incidents as they are taking place, much less prevent them.

On another note, some school administrators said they felt they had to control their behaviors because video surveillance cameras did not only see students but teachers and administrators as well. For example, Mr. Miller, one of the deans at Lincoln, said his relatively higher position in the regime of surveillance does not shield him from the cameras—in fact he said, the opposite is true. Because he is high up on the totem pole he feels compelled to act properly and be a role model:

> Sometimes I'm in the hallway and there are kids hanging out. Then I stop and think, there are cameras here, and I should say something to these kids, like 'Let's move' or something. Or sometimes I tell myself 'Don't pick up your nose or whatever, the camera's there.' That wouldn't reflect well on an administrator.

Mr. Casey, the assistant principal at Jefferson High, also made a similar point:

> I must tell you that at times I have to remind myself 'Hey, don't do something nutty.' I gotta tell you that I've forgotten about [the cameras] but every once in a while it pops in my head. Like, 'Hey, I better watch myself.' We have skirmishes sometimes with students. At times it's physical. There are times when students push me, and I respond. I push them back. I wouldn't feel very comfortable with that kind of thing being taped. It might be taken out of context. It's in the context of the situation, because we have an unusual interaction with these students. For example, I might curse freely at times around students but since I don't curse at them they are OK with it. However if someone heard that they would probably say that I was out of line and report it.

Students' Constructions of Video Surveillance

Students I interviewed at Jefferson High, like those in Lincoln Middle School, accounted for the presence of surveillance cameras from the perspective of safety and discipline. Dipka, a senior, emphasized the safety dimension, and noted: "They say it's for our safety. Now with situations like Columbine, you never know. So it's for our safety." Eric, also a senior, focused on discipline, and framed the surveillance system as a message from the administration to the students not to break the rules:

> It's good to have a camera. It's safe to have a camera. If there was no camera we would break the rules. That's why they put the cameras. So you can't break the rules. It's not bad. I am not looking at it like they are trying to scare us. I am looking at it as they are saying 'Don't break the rules.'

Like most Lincoln students who described video surveillance as a safety tool, Jefferson students too emphasized the benefits of surveillance and portrayed it in positive terms. Interestingly, even students who were caught on tape said favorable things about surveillance. For example, Cole, an 18-year old senior, said that authorities use surveillance cameras out of their concern for students. Cole was caught on camera early in the year while entering the building from the back door. He was reprimanded for his action, and in our interview he expressed some concern about being under surveillance, even though he said he is not personally tracked by the cameras:

> Cameras put a little stress on you. Yes, it does. To know that people are watching you. Watching your every single move. Stressed out like, what are these here for anyway?

Then he found the answer:

> In the long run when you think of it…they're here actually to protect us. Now we have to be protected in school. I could have been an intruder coming into the school to do something that shouldn't be done. So they

> actually gave me a little more confidence in the security of the school. With them having the cameras and with them staying on top of stuff. I see it as something good because it's helping us out. Protecting us. It makes me safe and it makes me uncomfortable. I don't really know.

A similar ambivalence also transpired in my interview with Adam, a 17-year-old senior who was caught on camera while talking on his cell phone. Adam was deeply resentful about the incident and angry with the administrators. He compared the school to a "jail," and called security agents "assholes." However, like Cole, he approved of the surveillance apparatus:

> They are doing it to protect us. You understand? They're looking out for our well being so that we can have a steady work environment, a learning environment. I don't like being on camera. But it's helping you out in the long run. Keeping you safe. It shows that the place is safe; it shows that they're watching out.

Like most students at Lincoln, these students at Jefferson also have a favorable opinion of video surveillance, which is primarily shaped by school administrators' discourse on the benefits of cameras. Mr. Smith said that they tell students "there is no reason for them to worry about the cameras if they behave like good citizens and carry themselves in a proper manner, in a proper fashion."

This statement exemplifies the prevailing language on surveillance on the part of administrators, which is circulated in the discursive space of the school. Students are told that there is nothing sinister about surveillance granted that you are not doing anything wrong. In this sense, it can be argued that those who assume power positions, school administrators in this case, establish a certain way of thinking and talking about video surveillance, and naturalize and normalize it. They speak of surveillance cameras as "security" cameras, and maintain that they use them out of concern for the safety of the students and the staff. They point out that the use of video surveillance technologies is a way of showing that they care about school safety. In emphasizing the care motif, like their colleagues at Lincoln, they disseminate the benefits of video surveillance.

In students' construction of video surveillance as an acceptable safety tool, the theme of acclimatization was also evoked. Some students said they were used to the presence of cameras in other public places, and therefore were not surprised to see them in the school. As Cole said:

> When I'm around cameras, I look at the camera and keep on walking. They have cameras at my mother's [housing] project. They put a system of cameras because there were bums that come into the apartment, and they would sleep in the hallways and nobody would see nothing. So now, they have cameras in there.

Jennifer, also a senior, illustrated the same point when she talked about cameras in department stores and delis:

> They are everywhere now. Like sometimes we go to the city with my girlfriends and they have'em at Macy's. It's for shoplifting. So it makes sure you don't steal. And in the school, it makes sure you don't do something crazy. Like I don't know hit someone. We also have it in my corner deli. The owner wants to protect his store from gangs I guess.

The presence of surveillance cameras in housing projects, retail stores, neighborhood delis, subway stations and other places students frequent in their everyday lives has already primed them for cameras in the school. To most students, the school is just another place where the cameras are in action. They see video surveillance systems as part and parcel of everyday life. As Kevin, a 10th grade students explains,

> [Video surveillance] is a common thing now. Cameras are everywhere. Almost every possible place you can go now. Shopping, the movies, the mall, anywhere… it's a part of society now. It's for catching the criminals. It's acceptable to me.

Video Surveillance as Prevention: Failure?

As this empirical analysis has shown, video surveillance systems do not necessarily succeed in deterrence or prevention. They can be effective in catching students after they commit a violation but they fail to turn students into "little angels." They do not stop students from fighting in the hallways, smoking in the backyard or cutting class.

Through administrators' and students' constructions, the institutional arrangements of video surveillance systems in schools reveal their shortcomings, failures and unforeseen consequences. While some students say they do not behave any differently just because they are under surveillance, others speak of the thrill or the fame one gets from being caught on camera or their acclimatization to cameras in other public settings.

Based on these findings, it becomes clear that most students do not care about being under surveillance—at least not to the extent that they are discouraged from breaking the rules or encouraged to observe them. It can be argued that video surveillance programs in the two schools studied here do not entirely resonate with the Panoptic model that Foucault discusses.

In *Discipline and Punish*, Foucault uses the Panopticon as a metaphor to allude to the subjectification of individuals in modern society through social control mechanisms operating through surveillance. He writes that the feeling of visibility and the uncertainty as to if or when one is being watched leads the individual to internalize the gaze of the watcher and to affect changes on himself. This, Foucault argues, is the ultimate goal and feat of Panoptic surveillance: producing docile bodies without any external coercion, thus assuring the automatic functioning of power. Foucault explains:

> He who is subject to a field of visibility, and knows it, assumes responsibility for the constraints of power, he makes them play spontaneously upon himself; he inscribes in himself the power relations in which he simultaneously plays both roles, he becomes the principle of his own subjection (1977, 202-3).

However, in Lincoln Middle School and Jefferson High School, video surveillance rarely makes students internalize prescribed ways of acting. Unlike the prisoners in the Panopticon, these students know who the inspector is and where the central watchtower is located, metaphorically speaking. Students know where the cameras are located and if the human observers are paying attention to surveillance footage.

Also, the watchers (deans, school safety agents) are highly visible and verifiable to students, unlike the inspector in the Panopticon. Further, students think that if they break the rules, they will not be caught on camera, and even if they are caught they will not be punished, since in their words "things slide." It is because of these reasons that the surveillance system does not induce a sense of permanent visibility and self-consciousness in students.

Surveillance inevitably brings up the problem of privacy, and we must explore how those who are subject to surveillance make sense of privacy in light of the presence of cameras in schools. This is the subject matter of the following chapter.

Notes

[1] It must be remembered that benefits of video surveillance (such as protection from bullies) generally exist in a somewhat hypothetical realm, and that the students (much less the administrators) cannot really know whether surveillance prevents danger, violence or misconduct.

[2] See Whitaker 1999, Staples 2000, Lyon, 1994, 2001, 2003, 2007, Nock 2003, Hier and Greenberg 2006, Rule 2007.

CHAPTER 4

Understanding Privacy

One of the most telling moments of this study occurred when a high school senior, who was caught on tape for a minor transgression, told me that he did not mind being under surveillance. Surveillance cameras functioned to guarantee safety at school, he reasoned, adding, "You don't have privacy when you are in the school anyways."

This was one of many similar remarks made by most participants in this study: that people do not mind video surveillance in public settings nor see it as an invasion of privacy, because they argue surveillance works to the benefit of the common good and there is no expectation of privacy in public. For example, majority of the students I interviewed in Lincoln Middle and Jefferson High School thought video surveillance did not constitute privacy invasion. Of the thirteen students I interviewed, only one expressed concern over being watched at school, while two raised questions about surveillance and privacy in settings other than the school. Also, most of the private citizens I interviewed in Washington Square Park evoked well-known arguments about surveillance and privacy in public settings. They said that there is no expectation of privacy in public, and that if you are not doing anything wrong then you should not be worried about privacy invasion. Of the sixteen park users I interviewed, only three of them expressed concern. A detailed discussion of these constructions can be found on following pages.

In this chapter, I make no claims to a universal conclusion about the surveillance/privacy problem, but rather offer insight into this topic through examination of actual, lived experiences of privacy.[1] I attempt to expand our understanding of privacy by addressing the following questions: Why do individuals say they are not worried about privacy invasion vis a vis video surveillance? In what settings or contexts do they say surveillance can be justified? How do they distinguish between private and public space? How do they talk about privacy and privacy invasion? And what are the dynamics that inform their thinking?

Constructions of the Surveillance/Privacy Nexus

Most students and park users do not consider the use of video surveillance in schools or in public parks as leading to privacy invasion. Based on my findings from in-depth interviews with these individuals, I identify three factors that play a role in this construction, and explain them below. They are: prioritization of the public interest over personal privacy, association of privacy with secrecy, and association of privacy with the personal or the familial realm.

The concept of the public interest

In portraying video surveillance as a safety tool that serves the common good, people generally refer to the benefits of video surveillance. One of the participants in this study, Tom, for example, talked approvingly of video surveillance although he had been caught on camera by the police. An unemployed African-American male in his mid-forties, Tom said he comes to Washington Square Park to be in "an environment where there's a little peace… to relax my mind, for a little tranquility, sometimes to smoke a joint." He talked about a time when he was smoking a joint in the park, and the cameras "saw me and the next thing I know I was in central booking. I got a tap on my shoulder saying, 'Guess what, we need you to come with us. We have you on surveillance.' They watched me roll up a joint." Despite this experience, Tom, a father of an eight-year-old girl, contended that surveillance cameras can be used for "good purposes:"

> This is a place a lot of people come. Too many people in one spot. Anything can happen to a person. God forbid. Kids walking around. A child can be abducted from a certain spot

> at a certain time. [The police] can rewind that [surveillance] tape back. So it also can be used as a blessing as well.

In referring to the benefits of surveillance, individuals also invoke the concept of public interest, and argue that it prevails over personal privacy concerns. For example, according to Jane, a white mother in her thirties who comes to Washington Square Park on a regular basis with her daughter, cameras are beneficial to public safety because they help the police to "watch out" for the public. According to Jane, the value of video surveillance in serving the public interest outweighs any privacy invasion claim:

> I see it as a positive thing. Not as negative. Not as privacy invasion. It doesn't bother me. I don't feel that [surveillance] is done with malice [to spy on people]. I mean isn't it great that somebody is keeping an eye out to make sure nothing goes awry? That there is somebody that could act to help me and help everybody who is there if something happens? I think that in the long run it protects people. Just because a few people are bothered by it doesn't mean it is invasion. It saves someone from being mugged. It's a good thing.

These comments resonate with privacy scholar Simon Davies' (1998) argument that privacy and public interest are in perpetual competition, and that privacy is typically portrayed as "an individual value that can be relinquished for the sake of collective concerns and the greater good" (145). Often represented through shocking events such as the Columbine shootings or through social problems such as drug trafficking that have negative effects on people's sense of safety and security, the concept of public interest constitutes a strong basis to render privacy implications as the cost of a trade-off between the common good and personal interests. As Jane and Tom argue, when the (supposed) benefits of video surveillance for the public interest are weighed against its (supposed) privacy implications, it is the former that prevails over the latter.

Amitai Etzioni (1999) also writes about the need for a balance between individual desires for privacy and collective needs. Etzioni warns against negative consequences that might occur if or when privacy is treated as sacrosanct and is privileged over collective concerns. Through an examination of public policies regarding the HIV-testing of infants and privacy of mothers; Megan's Law which discloses a convicted sex offender's presence in a given community; the government monitoring of encrypted communications; and the use of biometrics and national ID cards, Etzioni argues that a new conception of privacy is required that takes account of concerns for the common good. Etzioni suggests that people should recognize the significance of public safety, and entrust the community (friends, neighbors, members of voluntary associations) with the scrutiny of their behavior for the greater good. In doing so, Etzioni argues, people will not think that their privacy is invaded since they will be protecting collective interests and it will be their neighbors or friends undertaking the surveillance functions of the police or the government (213-215).

Association of privacy with secrecy

The second factor that shapes constructions of privacy has to do with the association of privacy with secrecy to hide some sort of misconduct or transgression. At Lincoln Middle and Jefferson High, for example, administrators and students I interviewed maintained that if a person is complaining about invasion of privacy, s/he must have done something wrong. According to Adam, a high school senior who was caught on tape while talking on his cell phone, "if you're doing something wrong, then you would probably say, 'yeah it's invading my privacy.' Of course, that's because you're doing something wrong really." On the other hand, Julia, an eight- grade student at Lincoln Middle said,

> I am used to cameras. I know what I'm doing. And if I were out there doing wrong, yeah I would worry about the cameras. I don't worry about them, because I know I'm not doing wrong.

Meanwhile, referring to possible privacy concerns on the part of teachers, Mr. Casey, the assistant principal at Jefferson High said,

> If you haven't done anything wrong, why would you worry about something like that? If a teacher is standing in the hallway and doing something that is not quite professional, when it's caught on camera then he's not going to feel confident about it, he's going to say, 'my privacy is being invaded' or something.

In Washington Square Park, both the police officers and park users brought up the similar I'm-not-doing-anything-wrong-then-why-should-I-be-worried argument (There was one participant, Vanessa, who did not agree. Her construction is discussed below).

For example, Jim, a white male in his thirties who comes to Washington Square Park to walk his dogs, said "If you aren't doing something wrong you have nothing to worry about the cameras. They watch you, big deal." Another park visitor, Monica, an African-American babysitter in her fifties, noted that she never really worries about the cameras because she never does anything that would get her in trouble.

One of the police officers I interviewed made a similar argument:

> If you're not doing anything wrong, then who cares who's watching you? You don't think about it after a while. You don't even know that they're there. You just go about your business.

An important point to keep in mind regarding these constructions is that participants are indicating that the surveillance system in question is not used to target a specific person, but rather to monitor the given public space and all the persons within it. They explain that they are not specific targets of surveillance cameras (since they are not doing anything wrong) and therefore they are not worried. As Julia said, "It's not only watching me. It's watching everybody." If she were specifically targeted then "yeah, I would be worried. But I'm not doing anything to attract special attention."

Association of privacy with the personal realm

The third factor that shapes conceptualizations of privacy as something not to be expected in public settings is its association with the personal or familial realm. Most students I interviewed equated privacy with seclusion, and contended that "privacy means like when you go to the bathroom make sure that nobody can see you," or "privacy is nobody else knows about your stuff."

For example, Katy, an eight-grade student I interviewed in Lincoln Middle, said she didn't "see anything wrong with [cameras in the school]" because the school is "a public space, not a private space." She added, "as long as they are not in the bathroom, it's OK." Cole, a senior at Jefferson High, identified privacy with the home, and said, "If they put cameras in your home, then something is wrong. But at school, it's OK because it's public."

Similar constructions emerged in the interviews I conducted with park visitors in Washington Square Park. Monica said, "privacy for me is being in my home with no one else around so I can just do whatever I want. Because nobody is watching, nobody is going to make judgments." In a similar vein, Jim noted, "if you want privacy you have it in your home." Jane said people might be concerned about privacy invasion if cameras were used in "a dressing room or a locker room, but if [they] are just out in public places, like the park, then they shouldn't be worried," and offered the following explanation:

> I don't feel like cameras are in any way taking away my privacy or freedom, because if you are in a public space, you are not private anyway. I don't understand how there could be any idea that you can have privacy in a public space. Because when you are in public, that's it: you are in public, not private.

The idea that one cannot expect privacy in a public space resonates with the association of privacy with the personal or the private sphere of the home.

There is a large body of work that focuses on the conceptual dichotomy between the private and the public. This dichotomy holds that the term "private" generally refers to the realm of familial and other personal or intimate relations, whereas "public" indicates the civic realm outside the personal one, or government institutions as opposed to private citizens or private institutions. As such, many philosophical and legal works argue for the protection of privacy of intimate or personal realms against intrusion by government or others, and thus assume an opposition between the private and the public (Nissenbaum 1998, 567-70).

This dichotomy tends to cast privacy purely as an individual value and thus at odds with collective interests. In regards to video surveillance, it is generally believed that surveillance cameras might create inconvenience for a few people whereas its benefits are enjoyed by the many. Jane's conceptualization of the balance between public safety and personal privacy exemplifies this attitude best:

> You need to think about the inconvenience that one person has versus the general good. You have to think of the public good, you have to think about where is the maximum gain and compare it to the inconvenience that this one person has because of cameras.

These interpretations of privacy can be explained through the presupposition that social life is divided into distinct private and public spheres, the "private sphere being a realm of individual decision making about sex, reproduction, marriage and family" (Allen 1999, 724). The classical organization that the private coincides with the home, the family and nonpolitical intimate associations generally conjures two kinds of imagery where the private can be contrasted with the public: 1. private is what is hidden or withdrawn versus what is open, accessible or revealed; 2. private is what is individual, or pertains only to an individual, versus what is collective, or affects the interests of a collectivity of individuals (Weintraub 1997, 5).

Privacy as a Contextual Value

Thus far I have explored how students and park visitors conceptualize privacy, and discussed the factors that play a role in these conceptualizations. Most of the time, individuals do not consider video surveillance as invasive or intrusive since they prioritize public safety benefits of video surveillance over its potential negative effects on privacy, and associate privacy with secrecy, isolation or the private sphere of the home.

These constructions can also be used to direct attention to the contextual nature of privacy. General theories of privacy provide significant insights into the problem of privacy but tend to overlook context-relative factors. In her theory of contextual integrity, Nissenbaum (2004) notes that we must pay attention to the nature of the context or the situation where a surveillance method is used, and examine the nature of the information extracted in that context, the roles of the agents receiving that information, their relationships to subjects, and the terms of sharing that information with others (137-38).

In order to establish whether a particular form of public surveillance (the monitoring of individuals in public through video, or data surveillance) leads to privacy invasion, Nissenbaum argues that we must analyze values and norms that govern relationships, practices and actions in a given context. There are two norms that help to shed light on whether the use of surveillance cause privacy invasion or not.

The first is norms of appropriateness, which dictate what kind of information about individuals is appropriate to reveal in a given context. In particular situations, the revelation of some kinds of information is expected or demanded. For example, while it is appropriate for a physician to ask for personal health information from his/her patients, the same is not true for an employer and his/her employees.

The second is norms of distribution which govern the transfer or movement of information from one party to another or others. Nissenbaum explains that in the context of friendship for example, norms of distribution are breached when one person divulges the other's personal information to a third party for reasons having nothing to do with the friendship. In terms of data surveillance, norms of distribution are violated if the agency engaged in the collection of health information to serve insurance companies, distributes this information to a third party for reasons other than insurance or healthcare. In this case, it can be argued that there is an invasion of privacy because the norm of distribution has been breached (Nissenbaum, 120-24).

The theory of contextual integrity is useful because it enables us to go beyond axiomatic claims about privacy invasion and take notice of privacy as a contextual construct. As many privacy scholars have shown, the meaning of privacy varies from place to place, culture to culture and period to period (Nissenbaum, 138). Privacy and social participation are competing desires, and the balance of privacy and disclosure is influenced by cultural norms and a particular individual's status and life situation (Westin 1967, 39). Privacy is about a continual "personal adjustment process in which [the individual] balances the desire for privacy with the desire for disclosure and communication of himself to others, in light of the environmental conditions and social norms set by the society in which he lives" (Westin, 7).

Contextual norms, environmental conditions and social participation dynamics help us understand why students and park visitors interviewed in this study are rather comfortable with video surveillance and not concerned about its implications on privacy and autonomy.

Notions of Control, Autonomy and Dignity

In talking about how they make sense of video surveillance in schools and public parks, most participants in this study directed attention to a possible trade-off between public safety and personal privacy. However, there were also participants who found video surveillance problematic even in public settings. Although few in number, they assessed the use of video surveillance in schools and public parks in negative terms, because they argued that it has a gender and race bias, and they maintained that video surveillance undermines autonomy and dignity and therefore violates privacy.

Gender and race

Bringing to light the role of human observers in shaping the use of cameras, two women in their twenties referred to feelings of objectification by the male gaze of the surveillance system in Washington Square Park. Kaitlin, a 29–year-old advertising executive, who lives in the neighborhood and on weekends meets her friends in the park, initially said that she doesn't think twice about the cameras in the park because "there can be a camera anywhere. It's just always there. Just because it's so engrained in our lives, it's something that you get used to. In the park, it's not like I'm doing anything that needs surveillance." Nonetheless, she said she felt uncomfortable thinking that a male police officer might be watching her:

> It's kind of a creepy feeling to think that maybe some guy, wherever...you don't even know who it is...can be sitting there watching you. Looking at you like he's not supposed to. It's kind of an eerie feeling. It doesn't affect the way that I do things, or change what I am doing. But it's just that same kind of thing where it's always in the back of your mind.

In a similar vein, Regina, a 27-year-old graduate student who attends New York University and therefore is in or around the park almost every day, said she gets a "funny" feeling from being watched by someone—probably a male—she does not know:

> It just bothers me…I get a little suspicious sometimes and paranoid and I try to find [the cameras]. I wonder if I'm being watched at that moment. It's scary. Right now is someone watching me that I have no idea about? And I always wonder what they're looking at in there, in that [police] van. I wonder do they just watch you walk through the park? I feel like maybe they are looking at me, as a woman. I'm being objectified.

Surveillance studies scholar Sheila Brown (1998) notes that it is generally assumed women welcome video surveillance because cameras theoretically enhance their feelings of safety in public spaces (207). In the case of Washington Square Park, this might be true for women like Jane, the mother who brings her daughter to the playground, but apparently not for others like Kaitlin and Regina. As Brown argues, for some women being watched by surveillance cameras does not create a feeling of safety; much less protect them from muggers, stalkers, rapists. To the contrary, Brown says, video surveillance might lead to anxiety for some: "Being seen, for women, is a condition of everyday life: their feelings of extreme visibility in public are created by masculine regulation of the public domain. Their exaggerated visibility creates insecurity" (208).

Kaitlin and Regina do not approve video surveillance because of the possibility—even if a slight one—that male police officers could be sitting in front of monitors and leering at them. For these women, video surveillance only adds to an already existing problem of visibility—visibility of women and the male gaze.

In addition to the gender problematic, another issue that came up in the interviews was the (supposed) race bias. Some African-American participants said they believed surveillance cameras specifically target them because of their skin color. For example, Derek, an African-American male in his thirties brought up this point as he unveiled his qualms about surveillance. He argued that "[the police] are paying more attention to [him] than white people:"

> One day I came here with a friend. And he dresses in baggy jeans and some boots. One day we were standing over here, and a cop came up and said we seen you discussing something on the camera. They thought we were buying and selling. I was searched. I was very angry at that moment. So I felt at that moment that my rights were being violated. So when I do come here, I feel like I'm being watched because I'm Black, you know.

During the interview, Derek repeatedly explained that he comes to Washington Square Park just to hang out, not to sell drugs, and tried to distance himself from the stereotypical perception of African-American males as drug dealers. He said: "That's all I really do. I just hang out. I've known these guys here for years. I play chess here. I don't sell drugs." Derek's initial apprehension to talk to a white person about surveillance cameras is understandable. When I approached him to ask if he would participate in a research study about cameras in the park, Derek's response was "Are you a cop?" Knowing about the presence of plain-clothes officers in the park, he was guarded about talking to me. It was only after I painstakingly convinced him that I was not a police officer, Derek started to talk about his experiences.

The claimed pre-selection of targets for surveillance based on skin color was also manifest in the interviews I had with Adam and Cole, seniors at Jefferson High. Although they were not troubled by surveillance in the school, surveillance in other public settings was loaded with meaning for these young African-American males. Adam said:

> Last week me and my cousin we went to a store in Manhattan, a Caucasian store. And wherever we went in the store the camera moved with us; it was moving with us to watch us because of our dark skin. Now that's not right. But in the school, it's for protection, and it is not just watching you like in the store. It is for everyone.

Cole echoed:

> In the school, principals and teachers need to be on top of things. So if principals, school counselors think they need cameras to make it a safe school, then so be it. The cameras in the stores, they bother me. Cause they think you are going to steal. Because you are Black. In the store, the camera means a lack of trust because of your color.

When Adam says cameras in the school do not bother him because they are for everyone, the racial/ethnic make-up of his school certainly comes into play. The student body at Jefferson High is predominantly African-American, South Asian and Hispanic. Here, white students are in the minority. So when Adam says the cameras are for everyone, he knows he is not being singled out because of his skin color. But it is a very different experience for him in a store in Manhattan that he describes as a "Caucasian" store. Although he knows he has not done "anything wrong" and has not drawn attention to himself by his behavior, he says he is treated as a potential criminal, as a possible threat. He feels he is not wanted. He is an outsider. He cannot be trusted. He says he has these feelings because "the minute I step into the store the camera I look at the camera and sometimes see it moving with me. Like following. Like I've done something."

In this study, I did not have the opportunity to interview or observe police officers or system operators who are directly responsible for operating the surveillance cameras in Washington Square Park or in the schools. Therefore, I cannot draw conclusions regarding the (supposed) gender and race biases claimed by participants. I must also note that these claims could be due to the fact that some individuals are more wary of surveillance and sensitive to its effects. Nonetheless, I still find it important to bring to light how Kaitlin, Regina, Derek, Adam and Cole make sense of surveillance, and think that these constructions warrant further exploration of how system operators' racial and/or gender biases might play into the selection and monitoring of specific individuals or population groups.

In England, criminologists Clive Norris and Gary Armstrong (1999) interviewed and observed police officers who operate surveillance cameras, and found that when the watchers target potential candidates for surveillance they utilize their existing understanding of who is most likely commit a crime or be troublesome. For example, system operators focus on the young rather than the old, disproportionately target blacks rather than whites, men rather than women, and the working rather than middle classes. In a similar vein, in his ethnographic research Benjamin Goold (2004) found that CCTV operators in police-led programs showed a strong bias towards the targeting of blacks, and young, white males (156-163).[2]

In response to arguments that the specific targeting of such groups merely reflects the underlying reality of the distribution of criminality, Norris and Armstrong write that the "production of the official statistics is also based on pre-given assumptions as to the distribution of criminality which itself leads to the particular configuration of formal and informal operational police practice" (119).

The guarantees that video surveillance systems do not deliberately monitor people are an empty rhetoric to African-American males. Their everyday, lived experiences refute the watchers' assertion that the camera is a neutral tool that sees everyone, not just African-Americans or people of other ethnicities.

Video surveillance is not color blind, and as John Fiske (2002) notes, the camera does not merely follow the laws of optics and electronics, but those of discourse and social norms. The technological process operates within the boundaries of social determinants of race: "To be seen to be Black or Brown… is to be seen to be out of place, beyond the norm that someone else has set, and thus to be subject to white power," Fiske writes (385).

This out-of-placeness is best illustrated by Jane, the (white) mother, who says of the African-American men sitting at the chess tables in Washington Square Park:

> I just get the feeling that they are people just hanging out. They don't seem to have a purpose. It seems like they are possibly homeless people, just sort of hanging out, and it's not elderly people watching the pigeons. The other thing is that...I hate to bring up the race component, but I do think to a certain extent that you have a lot of sort of Rastafarian guys hanging out. It does stand out as a pocket in the greater Village community.

The operation of video surveillance depends on norms, for without them it cannot identify the abnormal. It is through the norms that the watchers decide what (visual) information should be turned into knowledge and what individuals should be monitored (Fiske, 385).

In their study, Norris and Armstrong have identified the "working rules" that police or security officers exercise while operating video surveillance systems. Among these working rules, which are indeed manifestations of what the watchers consider normal and abnormal, are the following: 1) Operators target those who, in their understanding, are most likely to commit crime or be troublesome, and they are the youth, and particularly the male youth wearing track suit bottoms, baseball caps, football shirts, loose fitting jackets, etc, and young females seen with these male youth, ethnic minorities and blacks. 2) Operators focus on certain activities and actions that appear, in their judgment, out of place and out of time, for example, a group of young people congregating in an unusual location or cruising the streets in early morning. 3) Operators see those who treat the presence of cameras as other than normal as morally suspect and worthy of surveillance. For example, a person or a group of persons changing direction, backtracking or moving out of camera view are considered to have malign intent (119-149).

The gaze of the surveillance apparatus is about power relationships, which mostly revolve around definitions of what is normal and what is not. The attitudes, biases, prejudices, predispositions of the watchers shape the level of intrusiveness, the specifics of how particular groups are targeted and the precise aim of monitoring (Haggerty 2006).

In Aaron Doyle's (2006) words,

> Surveillance is not simply the capacity to watch but rather the capacity to define what's under consideration. The knowledge produced by surveillance cameras always involves interpretation (211).

Autonomy and dignity

In the preceding section, I have probed individuals' concerns about video surveillance from the perspective of (supposed) gender and race bias. In this study, some participants also criticized video surveillance in terms of how it undermines autonomy and dignity leading to invasion of privacy. For example, Kim, an eight-grader in Lincoln Middle School, expressed her frustration with the ubiquity of surveillance cameras (Kim was the only student in this study to bring this up). In Kim's judgment, surveillance cameras made her uncertain as to if, when and/or where she is being watched. Asked why, Kim replied:

> Everybody is looking at you. You feel funny. You feel strange. I don't know. You can't have peace to yourself because they're watching you. But sometimes you don't want people looking at you. Sometimes you just want to be in your own mind or whatever, and… you just want be yourself.

Kim's words speak to the idea of autonomy, the ability and the authority to withdraw oneself from the scrutiny of others, an important dimension of privacy.

In his analysis of the implications of information gathering modalities on privacy, Reiman (1995) argues that individuals who know that they are being observed or have a feeling of being visible do not belong to themselves. Surveillance "drains individual sovereignty away," and turns individuals into the data of the whole complex of information-gathering modalities. This in turn has significant implications for the self. As individuals grow up and live in what Reiman calls the "informational panopticon," they will be "less likely to acquire selves that think of themselves as owning themselves. They will say mine with less authority, and yours with less respect" (39-40). This also resonates with Beate Rossler's (2005) definition of privacy from the perspective of the individual: "Something counts as private if one can control the aces to this 'something.' Conversely, the protection of privacy means protection against unwanted access by other people." (8)

Personhood and privacy are interconnected. Privacy is a precondition for personhood, because the individual cannot shape his /her destiny without recognizing that s/he has the actual capacity and the moral right to do so. Therefore, s/he needs to believe and know that his/her destiny in a moral sense belongs to her. Through privacy, the society or the social group in question can demonstrate and confirm the respect for that person (Reiman, 310, 313).

This point is also illustrated by Vanessa, a 25-year-old office manager who comes to Washington Square Park for her lunch break. Unlike many others I interviewed in the park, Vanessa gets upset about cameras in public spaces merely because of the fact that she is being watched (Vanessa was the only participant in Washington Square Park to mention this point):

> There's a camera down in the tunnel in the PATH station and every time I go by it, I jump and I smack it. Every single time. Or, I give it the finger. It's ridiculous, because it's a machine. I'm flipping it off and it's a machine. There's something about its presence and the fact that someone, somewhere, thinks that they have a right to watch me as I come through that tunnel, for whatever purpose they want to watch me. It doesn't matter if I'm not doing anything wrong. I have a right to go through that tunnel without being watched and the fact that I am being watched makes me angry.

I do not wish to fetishize these accounts and argue that they reflect general concerns. They seem idiosyncratic against the backdrop of the majority of remarks that are accepting of video surveillance, yet I think they are valuable in pointing our attention to dimensions of the privacy problem that are often neglected in public debates.

One of these dimensions is dignity. To have privacy means that individuals can communicate their intimate thoughts without having their dignity threatened (Fortner 1986, 156) Dignity is important, because it is an inherent aspect of humanness, not bestowed by one upon another, not created or earned. However, it can be stripped away or diminished by others. And it is privacy that gives the individual the opportunity to think through her actions, alter herself and determine who she is. As Vanessa makes clear:

> What about my right as a human being to live and to exist without being monitored? That's it. I don't even think that requires any justification. "Well, I don't do anything wrong." No! What about my given human dignity? My right, as a human being, to live my life without being observed by people who claim and purport to have authority over me.

These narratives strike a chord with James Rule's (2007) discussion of privacy as basic to personhood. Rule notes that every human being holds rights to elementary dignity and independence, which can be eroded by unauthorized monitoring and use of personal information. Based on Kantian principles (that persons must be recognized as ends and that their most fundamental interests cannot be overridden for the happiness or welfare of all), Rule argues that people should have the right to a significant measure of control over their personal information—a right as basic as the right not to be enslaved or the right to personal property (187).

Another philosophical dimension of privacy that is not included in public debates has to with personal autonomy. Autonomy and its promotion are individual goals facilitated by privacy.

Privacy promotes liberty of action because it shields us from interference and ridicule (Gavison 1980, 448). It is easier to be autonomous in "an open society committed to pluralism, toleration, and encouragement of independent judgment rather than blind submissiveness." However, regardless of how open the society is, it is likely that behaviors that deviate from social norms will be subject to sanctions. The possibility of sanctions produces an inhibitive effect on the individual, therefore privacy is needed to enable the individual to deliberate and establish his opinions, in other words exercise his autonomy (450). As Regina says:

> I think that I have the right to determine what my own behavior should be and live my life the way I want to live it, as long as I am not hurting other people. I think that the cameras threaten that. I think that it threatens to set parameters for what is "correct behavior," which is such a subjective notion anyway.

Kaitlin echoes such concerns, adding that cameras make her angry because:

> What goes through my mind is, "Who are you? Who are you to say that you have a right to set the parameters for my behavior or dictate my behavior? I don't think a camera or anyone behind it has a right to determine how I should behave. It makes me feel like I'm 13 years old. That's exactly what it is.

Privacy: An Elusive Concept

These actual stories and words, and the diverse, specific, and contextual interpretations show how privacy takes on different articulations depending on the social context, the specific surveillance apparatus and power arrangements it deploys. In this light, it is imperative that we do not limit the discussion of the implications of surveillance technologies to the usual privacy invasion claims, but instead explore autonomy and dignity as crucial aspects of privacy.

General privacy invasion claims merely associate privacy with "the right to be let alone" and therefore hide more specific and substantive privacy needs and desires. This conception can be traced back to Samuel D. Warren and Louis D. Brandeis (1890), who directed attention to the problem of privacy as a legal concept. Prompted by the arrival of photography and the mass circulation of newspapers, particularly by yellow journalism that covered Mrs. Warren's parties in personal and embarrassing detail, Warren and Brandeis warned that the new technologies threatened "the right to be let alone... the right most valued by civilized man" (183). Warren and Brandeis did not define the right to privacy as the right to be alone, but rather implied that the right to privacy is a special case of the latter (Gavison, 437) and expressed the need for privacy to exist as a common law tort. Regrettably, this rather equivocal argument has been erroneously interpreted and long used as a sound-bite definition for privacy.

This abstract conception of privacy, which has taken quite a stronghold over privacy debates, ignores the very real relations of power and domination that are at work in the politics of surveillance. To refocus the surveillance-privacy nexus on a more engaging and vital debate, we must move questions about power and domination to the forefront and replace the "rights talk" with vernacular critiques made by those who are watched. We must take into account the diversity, particularity and context of surveillance practices and their implications for privacy (Gilliom, 2001 9, 119).

Another dimension of privacy that we need to consider has to do with values. Privacy has positive functions on part of both the individual and the society. It is beneficial to the individual because it restricts physical access, promotes liberty of action, autonomy and human relations; insulates the individual against ridicule and censure, and limits exposure to others.

On the other hand, privacy is valuable to the democratic society because it makes it possible for individuals to form judgments and express preferences autonomously, which is central to participation in political decisions (Gavison, 455). Such a conceptualization of privacy is not aligned with secrecy or isolation but with autonomy and agency. Further, we must recognize that absolute privacy is not desirable, and that individuals should be able to maintain a balance between accessibility and privacy. As Gavison notes, privacy fosters the moral autonomy of the citizen; it does not grant secrecy or absolute privacy to individuals. It helps individuals to grow, maintain their mental health, create and maintain human relations, and lead meaningful lives.

Notes

[1] Since the scholarly literature on privacy is simply too broad, I choose to direct readers' attention to some key works instead of presenting a detailed review. In *Privacy and Freedom* (1967), Alan Westin recognizes that privacy serves not only individual freedoms, but also broader social functions in liberal democracies, such as providing support for religious tolerance, scholarly investigations, serving the integrity of the electoral system, and limiting the police power. Oscar H. Gandy in his definitive work, *Panoptic Sort: A Political Economy of Personal Information* (1983), probes the outcomes of technological developments on privacy. Gandy contends that electronic surveillance and information gathering systems are determined by the play of tensions within late capitalism and the structures of the market. Gandy examines the political economy of the ability of organizations to monitor individuals, and defines the monitoring capabilities of institutions the "panoptic sort." He uses the term "panoptic" to draw on the inseparability of discipline, power and knowledge. Surveillance in general and the panoptic sort in particular assigns individuals to conceptual groups on the basis of identifying information, and then carries out a comparative classification of individuals in terms of measured attributes in order to establish norms of acceptability, Gandy argues. In *The Unwanted Gaze: The Destruction of Privacy in America* (2000), Jeffrey Rosen focuses on the gathering of personal information in cyberspace and discusses the threats posed by digital communications technologies. Rosen argues privacy protection cannot rely only on technological means but must involve legal, political safeguards. In a similar vein, Daniel Solove in *The Digital Person: Technology and Privacy in the Information Age* (2004) tackles the problem of privacy in

light of profound technological developments of the Information Age. Solove argues that the creation and implementation of digital dossiers (digital profiles of personal data gathered and used by databases) pose new threats to privacy and require a new understating of privacy as well as new protections. In *Privacy Lost: How Technology is Endangering Your Privacy* (2006), David Holtzman also explores the effects of digital world on privacy: emergence of networks destroys our ability to control information, and emergence of privacy-related crimes are result of computer technology. In discussing the legal basis for privacy protection, Holtzman calls for a balance between national security and privacy. A more complex view is presented by James B. Rule in *Privacy in Peril: How We are Sacrificing a Fundamental Right in Exchange for Security and Convenience* (2007), who directs attention to legal uses of personal information as opposed to illegal ones. In his advocacy for strong privacy protections, Rule tells us that to overcome endangerment of privacy we must first stop providing personal information for convenience or security. Readers interested in privacy-surveillance-technology nexus can also consult *Computers, Surveillance and Privacy* (Lyon and Zureik 1996), *Technology and Privacy: The New Landscape* (Agre and Rotenberg 1998), *The Transparent Society: Will Technology Force Us to Choose between Privacy and Freedom?* (Brin 1999), *Database Nation: The Death of Privacy in the 21st Century* (Garfinkel 2001), *Surveillance as Social Sorting: Privacy, Risk and Digital Discrimination* (Lyon 2003), *Global Surveillance and Policing: Borders, Security, Identity* (Zureik and Salter, 2005). Aside from the interplay between technology and privacy, another significant body of literature deals with privacy law. Scholars working in this field are generally concerned with the legal vacuum regarding the protection of privacy, and what should be done about it (Cate 1997, Doyle 1992, Alderman and Kennedy 1995.) Newman (2008) discusses the role of regulatory control in privacy protection, and documents how and why the European Union has adopted data privacy laws in public and private sectors. Directing attention to the important role regulatory capacity plays in regional and international politics, Newman argues that strong data privacy generates regulatory power and a strong standing in the global political economy. Although privacy literature is replete with calls for privacy protection and regulation, the actual experiences of privacy advocates have not been examined in-depth. This gap is filled by Bennett (2008) who explores the organization, resources and strategies of privacy advocates. Bennett provides an overview of civil society groups, actors within them, and dynamics of conflicts over privacy. Through interviews with privacy advocates, Bennett also documents how these actors resist surveillance technologies and fight for privacy protection. Literature on privacy law also offers perspectives into what should be done to achieve more and/or better privacy protection. Proposals generally include, but are not limited to, creation of more comprehensive privacy policy, proper enforcement of data protection, implementation of self-regulatory mechanisms, implementation of privacy impact assessments, application of privacy-enhancing technologies. In this vein, some noteworthy titles are: *Legislating Privacy: Technology, Social Values and Public Policy* (Regan 1995), *Surveillance, Privacy and the Law* (Gilliom 1996), *Visions of Privacy: Policy Choices for the Digital Age* (Bennett and Grant 1999), *Privacy in Peril* (Rule 2007), *The War on Privacy* (Klosek 2007), *Privacy: The Lost Right* (Mills 2008), *Protectors of Privacy: Regulating Personal Data in Global Economy* (Newman 2008), *The Privacy Advocates: Resisting the Spread of Surveillance* (Bennett 2008). Against this tide of scholarly examinations that call for better, stronger tools to protect privacy, Amitai Etzioni (1999) offers a distinct perspective. In *Limits of Privacy*, Etzioni focuses on the basic tension between the individual desire for privacy and the collective concern for health and safety issues, and asserts that negative consequences to society might occur when privacy is treated as sacrosanct, and therefore we need a new conception of privacy—one that recognizes concerns for the common good over privileging privacy a priori. Etzioni argues that there will be less public control when it is the friends, neighbors or fellow members of voluntary associations that scrutinize the behavior, as opposed to the police or secret agents. The informal social scrutiny mechanisms will reduce the need for government control, and such a communitarian approach to privacy will take into consideration the common good and sociohistorical changes (213-215). In a similar vein, David Brin in *The Transparent Society: Will Technology Force Us to Choose between Privacy and Freedom?* (1999) challenges the social and cultural assumptions surrounding the relationship between privacy and freedom, and claims that the proliferation of surveillance in its various incarnations is not a threat to freedom, but rather it is emancipatory. He explains that a society in which everybody, not just the rich and the powerful, has the ability to monitor, observe and watch one another is a transparent society, given that surveillance elicits accountability. Brin argues that the danger presented by surveillance is not its spread, but its usurpation by the few. Steven Nock joins Brin in turning long-held beliefs about privacy on their ear. In *The Costs of Privacy* (1993), Nock challenges the prevailing argument about the constant erosion of privacy over the course of the last two centuries.

Instead, he asserts that Americans have come to enjoy greater privacy, which has created a society of strangers that requires increased surveillance. Surveillance helps to establish and maintain reputations in such a society, enabling institutions and individual actors to trust strangers. Therefore, surveillance is not the cause of privacy invasion; it is the result of greater privacy. Nock argues that as members of society become more anonymous and private, surveillance —in the form of credentials (credit cards, driver's licenses) or ordeals (lie detectors, drug tests) —increases accordingly.

[2] Goold also examined local authority-led CCTV programs and found that CCTV operators in these schemes disproportionately focused on women--mostly for shoplifting related reasons (156).

CHAPTER 5

Conclusion

The major impetus behind this study is the need to investigate video surveillance historically and contextually paying special attention to socio-political dynamics behind its emergence and intensification, and to its social outcomes in terms of power, control and privacy. In this chapter, I summarize answers to research questions posed at the beginning, revisit the theoretical model of the Panopticon in light of the research findings gathered from the fieldwork, and discuss some areas of future research.

Socio-Political Forces behind Video Surveillance

The first research question I ask in this study has to do with the driving forces behind the generation and intensification of video surveillance programs in public settings. How do the watchers frame the concept of public interest and public safety in their accounts of the use of video surveillance? In what specific ways do they use surveillance cameras? What assumptions about deterrence and prevention inform their thinking?

In light of the review of literature on surveillance, social control and crime control, historical analyses of press reports, and findings from interviews with law enforcement officials and school administrators, I argue that the two broad socio-political dynamics that enable the generation and intensification of video surveillance programs in parks, streets and schools have to do with risk management and crime prevention. As I showed in Chapter 3, from the 1970s onwards the criminal justice system shifted its attention from rehabilitation of individual offenders to control and administering of whole populations.

This movement from rehabilitation to prevention was borne out of the failure of the rehabilitative approach that sought to reform offenders' mental dispositions and behaviors through incarceration (Garland 1996). Despite efforts to return offenders to the society as reformed individuals, the continuing presence of crime led law enforcement and the judicial system to seek out new approaches, crime prevention being the first and foremost. Aiming to deter potential offenders from engaging in wrongful acts in the first place, this new approach directed human and technological resources to the control of physical environments and the populations within them.[1]

Based on the interviews I conducted with school administrators and police officers, I argue that the use of video surveillance as a preventive strategy resonates with the above-discussed crime prevention model. Police officers, Department of Education officials, and school administrators explained that they use video surveillance systems to dissuade individuals (in this case, park visitors and students) from committing criminal acts or engaging in undesirable, disruptive behaviors in the first place. As one police officer noted, New York City Police Department's decision to install surveillance cameras in Washington Square Park was spurred by the need to prevent and/or reduce drug trafficking. NYPD's objective was (and still is) to affect changes on the behaviors of sellers and buyers (and others who might engage in dealing) by letting them know that cameras are monitoring their behaviors and that they are going to be apprehended if they sell or buy drugs.

In a similar vein, deterrence and prevention are the two primary objectives of video surveillance in school premises. School administrators seek to deter students from engaging in disruptive or violent behaviors, such as cutting class, roaming the hallways or fighting. Like law enforcement officials, school administrators are using cameras to make real the likelihood of apprehension should the students do "something wrong." As one assistant principal explained, the intended message is, "We have our eyes on you, so be on your best behavior."

This turn to preventive surveillance in schools is quite telling because it illustrates how strategies and technologies initially deployed in the field of crime control spill over to other domains of social life. Faced with large student populations, inadequate human resources, and broader social problems that lead to safety and discipline problems, school administrators embark on practices once reserved for the criminal justice system. From "zero tolerance" policy to deployment of uniformed officers, metal detectors and surveillance cameras, they adopt a wide range of anti-crime, anti-violence initiatives, and, knowingly or not, help establish a strict culture of control.

Experience of Video Surveillance in Specific Contexts

How do individuals experience video surveillance and the larger project of deterrence and prevention? Does the hypothesized success of video surveillance in deterrence and prevention necessarily translate into practice? To what extent does the theoretical model of the Panopticon help us to understand the effects of video surveillance on those who are watched? The objective of these questions is more than to evaluate specific video surveillance systems or to confirm/refute the watchers' arguments regarding their success in prevention. Instead, by way of addressing these questions, I want to propose that the specific context whereby cameras are used impinges on how individuals experience surveillance, and argue that any critical investigation of video surveillance should be grounded in contextual analysis.

In surveillance literature, references to and discussions of the Foucauldian theory of discipline and power that flow from the Panopticon are all too common. The tenor of Foucault's theory rests on social institutions' turn to surveillance as part of their effort to control certain segments of the population (criminals, consumers, workers, students, etc). Foucault (1977) contends that individuals in Panoptic institutions such as prisons, schools, barracks, hospitals, asylums and poor-houses internalize the given authority's power that stems from surveillance and are thus deterred from engaging in wrongful behavior. They become their own overseers guaranteeing the automatic and smooth functioning of the disciplinary mechanism (202-3).

While the Panoptic model offers a general understanding of surveillance, its effect and experience, it is imperative that we pay attention to the context where surveillance programs are deployed, and explore their particular configurations. We must be careful not to engage in across-the-board applications of the Panopticon, but instead analyze video surveillance systems in specific contexts addressing different modes of power they employ and different experiences of power, control and privacy they produce. What I offer in the following sections is such a contextual analysis of video surveillance in the school and in the public park.

Video Surveillance in Schools

In light of the fieldwork conducted in two New York City public schools, I argue that video surveillance does not always succeed in deterrence or prevention. Claims made by Department of Education officials that video surveillance changes students' behaviors in acceptable ways and thus prevents disorderly, dangerous, violent, or wrongful acts are unsubstantiated since there is no data to support them.

Further, these claims are questionable since students are generally indifferent to video surveillance and they do not change their behaviors in ways that are acceptable to the watchers. There are two reasons behind this phenomenon: First, students who are intent on behaving in a particular way do so regardless of the video surveillance system, by moving out of the cameras' view thus rendering themselves unobservable to system operators (security officers and assistant principals or deans). When they cut class or get into a fight, they choose to do so in areas that are not under surveillance. Second, and more importantly, the watchers are identifiable, and their actions observable to students. Students know that it is the assistant principal, the dean and/or the security officer who is engaged in the act of watching. Students are also well aware that often times the watchers do not pay due attention to monitors and surveillance footage. For example, students in Lincoln Middle School said, they can see that the security officers, assigned to the security console, are idling, chatting or eating lunch instead of looking at the surveillance footage. Students reason that since the human observers are not paying attention to the footage, they won't be caught on tape and/or punished for their behaviors.

Video surveillance in Washington Square Park

Washington Square Park offers an excellent case study on the installation of surveillance cameras as a crime deterrent. One can argue that the cameras have cleared the park from drug dealers and other petty criminals only to displace them to other areas. Where once drug trafficking took place in plain sight in the very center of the park, drug dealers now either seek out corners of the park screened by trees or move to adjacent streets where there aren't any cameras.

Since it was first installed, the video surveillance system in Washington Square Park has not so much prevented drug dealing as it has simply turned it into the problem of another neighborhood. In response, law enforcement officials continue to extend the surveillance apparatus to new locations. Local police officers interviewed for this study acknowledged that sellers and buyers simply moved out of the view of the cameras in Washington Square Park, and came to inhabit Grove Street, just a few blocks away. At the time of these interviews, the officers stated that the NYPD was planning to install cameras on Grove Street as well. Recent maps of surveillance cameras in New York City show that there are now four cameras on Grove Street.[2] In light of these findings, it can be argued that video surveillance moves crime from one location to another, and that it only begets more surveillance. Crime continues to exist, and the web of surveillance extends.

In this example, the video surveillance system deters or may deter drug dealers from dealing in the park but it does not deter them from dealing elsewhere; in other words, it does not reform or rehabilitate them as the Panoptic perspective would have us believe. Yet the surveillance system achieves a subtler goal. By identifying definitions of normal and deviant behavior, it reinforces the behaviors of the already law-abiding citizens. Park visitors I interviewed told me they have no reason to worry about being in a public setting that is under surveillance. They behave appropriately and lawfully, and they don't think about buying or selling drugs or committing unlawful acts. They are "not doing anything wrong" or anything worthy of surveillance. They say surveillance cameras—or rather the system operators—focus on individuals who display suspicious behaviors, not them. They also acknowledge that in this setting everyone and every behavior will be watched.

Further, video surveillance establishes parameters of acceptable and unacceptable behavior. Unlike the students I discussed above, park visitors cannot identify their watchers and they have no knowledge of how the watchers use the surveillance system. Park visitors cannot know whether they are under constant or only intermittent surveillance. Most regular park visitors know that the police van that is permanently stationed on the southeast corner of Washington Square Park is used as a "control room." For example, a park visitor said that "all those wires going into the van are the wires from the cameras" and added that it was obvious "they are watching the cameras in that van." But park visitors do not know when or if the police officers are watching the footage from the cameras. They do not know how many officers are in the van. They do not know what exactly the officers are looking at. In other words, the watchers are invisible and unverifiable to park users. As a female park visitor noted:

> I always wonder what they're looking at in there. I wonder, do they just watch you walk through the park? What if I'm being objectified or what exactly is going on in the truck? How many people are in there? It's not really open to the public and [what goes on inside] is not really known. I just wonder how many people don't realize that.

That the watchers are desubjectivized makes the surveillance system in Washington Square Park "effective" in the sense that it reinforces appropriate behaviors on the part of park visitors. The surveillance system's effectiveness derives in no small part on the invisibility of its monitors. The less verifiable the watchers are, and the less transparent their activities are, the more effective the system is, in the sense that individuals start to scrutinize their own behavior. It must be remembered that this effect is not necessarily on the deviant but on the normal.

Most individuals interviewed for this article stated that they have no reason to worry about cameras, because they said they behave appropriately and lawfully. They said they are "not doing anything wrong" or anything worthy of surveillance. For these individuals, surveillance cameras are used to monitor those who display suspicious behaviors or engage in unlawful acts, not law-abiding citizens like them. But they also noted that everyone and every behavior is watched in this process. As Jacques Ellul (1964) once commented, "to be sure of apprehending criminals, it is necessary that everyone be supervised" (100). Yet normal, law-abiding people expressed anxiety about the idea of being monitored. They were certain that they were under surveillance, but uncertain whether they were being singled out. This paradoxical experience is the consequence of the double entendre of video surveillance, that it watches each and all, both the normal and the deviant.

As the above comments indicate, individuals—regardless of whether they are doing anything wrong or not—start paying attention to their own behaviors and follow the parameters of acceptable and unacceptable behavior established by the authorities. They monitor their behaviors, and shun inappropriate, unwanted, unreasonable acts. By saying "I'm not doing anything wrong," they declare that they are following the norms.

Individuals start to pay attention to their own behaviors, becoming more aware that the police might interpret them as "suspicious" and invite the cameras to zoom in on them. How does a person behave or react should a known drug dealer sits next to him/her on the bench? What if a "suspicious-looking" character strikes up a conversation with a law-abiding individual? Does the individual become concerned that the surveillance system operator will assume that a drug transaction is taking place? These questions and concerns highlight the work of video surveillance on the "normal" and "docile" individuals. In their minds, video surveillance and the visibility it generates—being seen next to someone, for example— form the raw material for authorities to make decisions about individuals.

Surveillance fabricates individuals around institutionally established norms, and enables the institutions to govern at a distance, bolstering their authority (Ericson and Haggerty 1997, 450). In this sense, video surveillance can be situated as a governmental strategy that regulates the conduct of individuals at a distance.[3]

In light of these accounts, how can we make sense of the rationale for video surveillance systems and of their implications? What new theoretical insights can we offer that take into consideration varied experiences of surveillance, power and privacy? To this end, I turn to concepts of self-responsibilization and governmentality.

Video Surveillance, Self-Responsibilization and Governmentality

Foucault (1991) first offered the idea that governmentality encapsulates the shift in the exercise of power from negative, punitive governing to a more positive, productive outcome (92). Governmentality embraces the efficient and economical application of power; therefore, it requires not force, "wrath," or "a weapon of killing," but rather "wisdom and diligence." Wisdom, Foucault explains, is to be understood as the "knowledge of things, of the objectives that can and should be attained, and the disposition of things required to reach them," and diligence as "the principle that a governor should only govern in such a way that he thinks and acts as though he were in the service of those who are governed" (96). To rule individuals in a productive way, the government must "know the inside of people's minds, explore their souls, make them reveal their innermost secrets" (1983, 214).

In this light, the crux of governmentality is not the subjectification of individuals to some exemplary penalty, but rather their placement under surveillance, eliciting their participation to make themselves known without the use of force (Foucault 1972, 38). Subsequent literature on governmentality explores this particular mode of governing and the resultant self-disciplining of subjects within neo-liberal formations in late 20th century (Castel 1991, Rose 1996, Barry et al. 1996, Hay 2000, Ouelette 2004).

In one of the most useful elaborations on the topic, Nikolas Rose (1996) explains that neo-liberalism does not abandon the "will to govern;" instead, it seeks to invent new strategies, rationalities and techniques that will "create a distance between the decisions of formal political institutions and other social actors, and conceive of these actors in new ways as subjects of responsibility, autonomy and choice, and seek to act upon them through shaping and utilizing their freedom" (53-54).

As I discussed in Chapter 2, neo-liberalism has fostered, among other strategies, the replacement of the social citizen and a common society with the responsible individual and a self-governing community (Rose, 56). For the purposes of this discussion, I would like to focus on this dynamic, and position video surveillance as a mechanism that off-loads the responsibility of normalization through visibility and its maintenance to the individuals. The necessity to discourage disobedient acts as well to perpetuate the already-embodied normative behaviors articulated within the requirements of public safety and security make the individual visible to the gaze of the authority but more importantly to oneself.[4]

Video surveillance actually creates or enhances the sense of one's visibility. It thereby enables social institutions to throw off at least some of their responsibility to the individual, making the deterrent and disciplinarian mechanisms work more subtly and effectively. Video surveillance then assures the automatic functioning of power not because it reforms the deviant but because it integrates the normal into the "power situation of which they themselves are made to be the bearers" (Foucault 1977, 201).

As I showed in Chapter 2, law enforcement is paying increasing attention to the control of whole populations, constituting them as risks that must be continuously monitored to preempt undesirable behaviors. The primary objective of this deterrence initiative is to create defensible spaces or controlled environments that will discourage unlawful and violent acts. However, these risk-based initiatives are not simply projects of (crime) prevention; they are indeed projects of governance, conducting the conduct of individuals (to borrow Foucault's term).

Beyond the Panopticon

A significant factor that accounts for different experiences of surveillance in the school and in the park has to do with the "architecture" of the given space and the mode of power employed within it. The school is a bound environment with its Panoptic model of surveillance and is illustrative of Foucault's "disciplinary society," whereas the park is an unbound environment with a different model of power that evokes Gilles Deleuze's "society of control" (1992).

The school is a bound environment or a "space of enclosure" as Deleuze calls it (3), and can be associated with the Panopticon—the archetypal space of enclosure. According to Foucault, it is around these "spaces of enclosure" such as schools, workplaces, prisons, barracks, hospitals where the disciplinary society organizes and administers everyday life, and rules the population (3). As Deleuze explains, these "closed environments" rely on disciplinary mechanisms to "concentrate, to distribute in space, to order in time, to compose a productive force within the dimension of space-time whose effect will be greater than the sum of its component parts."

Deleuze reminds us that in these enclosed sites, discipline operates in a given time frame and is bound by spatial limits. However, this is not to suggest that the effect of discipline is also contained within institutional boundaries (temporal, spatial). In other words, the work of discipline does not end when the student finishes school or the prisoner is released from prison. While day-to-day operations are obviously time- and space-bound, their effects are not. Individuals pass from one space of enclosure to another (from family to school to barracks to the factory, and from time to time the hospital or the prison) rendering the effect of discipline continuous. Therefore, we must keep in mind that when Deleuze points to the spatial and temporal limits of discipline in enclosed environments, he is referring to the operation of discipline, not its effect.

The mode of power and control in the school resembles those in the Panopticon for a couple of reasons: first, students' presence in the school is non-voluntary. Students go to school because they have to. Their activities and movements are subject to certain restrictions, and their attendance is conditioned by a spatial/temporal structure (schedule of classes, curricular activities) over which they have no control. Their movements and activities are directed through both the architecture of the physical building and the temporal structure of the daily schedule. For example, students are required to be present at school between certain hours; they cannot come and go as they wish. There is controlled entrance and exit in and out of the building; the school perimeter is demarcated by walls or fences, and students are not allowed in certain areas without permission or at certain times. They cannot be in the hallways during class time without a "hall pass," and they can only go to the gym, library, cafeteria at designated times.

These disciplinary mechanisms that manage students in time and space have always been at work in the school; as a matter of fact, they are its defining characteristics. Being at school is being controlled, and the students are acclimated to it. Even before the introduction of surveillance cameras, students are already used to being watched, figuratively speaking. They are already accustomed to being disciplined and controlled by various mechanisms; therefore sensitivity to video surveillance on their part is low. In other words, because they have always been regulated and controlled, students do not consider video surveillance in the school as particularly problematic.

In contrast to the school, the public park is not a space of enclosure. It does not necessarily resemble the Panopticon, and the individuals within it experience video surveillance differently than the students in the school. The park is different from the Panoptic space of enclosure because it is an open, unbound space. Its premises are not walled up nor does it have an entrance, a checkpoint, etc. More importantly, park visitors' presence in the park is voluntary; they go to the park because they want to, not because they have to. And while in the park, they are not subject to a schedule; their movements and behaviors are not bound by a temporal/spatial structure.

In contrast to students, park visitors are not as restricted in their activities; they enjoy a relatively higher level of autonomy. But this is not to suggest that the park is a completely unregulated environment. For example, there are several rules that govern how individuals can use the park. In New York City, park visitors are prohibited from making disturbing noises, camping overnight, possessing alcohol, obstructing sitting areas, spitting. They can engage in bicycling, rollerblading, playing musical instruments or meetings only in designated areas or with permit. In addition to these overt control mechanisms, park visitors' behaviors may also be subject to discipline by subtler ones such as video surveillance. As discussed earlier, some visitors may become conscious of their behaviors as result of being watched by cameras, and pay attention to parameters of acceptable and unacceptable behavior. The visibility that stems from video surveillance in the park and the consequent calculation of behaviors on the part of park visitors signal a different, perhaps a softer disciplinary mechanism than the one employed in the school.

While the school resembles the Foucaldian disciplinary society with its hard mode of control in Panopticon-like sites, the park is more evocative of the Deleuzian society of control with its soft mode of control. I do not use the notion of the society of control to claim a strict parallel between it and the park, but to direct attention to the subtle nature of the disciplinary mechanisms that they both utilize. According to Deleuze, society of control, which is replacing the disciplinary society, relies on forms of free-floating control to administer populations (4, 6).

Unlike the disciplinary society, which concentrates control within institutions, society of control disperses it and operates through a network of institutions, spaces, experiences. In society of control, control is malleable. It takes on a new form in each environment, be it in a corporation or on a television show. Control is a modulation, not a mold, "that will continuously change from one moment to the other, or like a sieve whose mesh will transmute from point to point" (Deleuze 4).

Video Surveillance in Non-institutional Contexts

Varied moments or points of surveillance, outside the contexts of the school and the public park, must also be taken into consideration as we try to develop new theoretical frameworks for video surveillance. In this study, I have focused on the school and the park primarily because these were the sites I could gain access to. Yet it is common knowledge that video surveillance is now part of everyday life in workplaces, shopping malls, retail stores, restaurants, airports, banks, nursing homes, daycare centers. In these sites, cameras are supported, welcomed and encouraged for safety and security reasons –not just by the watchers but interestingly by the watched.

To better understand these moments and points of video surveillance, we need to turn away from the theoretical model of the total institution to that of the rhizome. Borrowing Deleuze and Guattari's (1987) concept of the rhizome, Ericson and Haggerty (2000) argue that contemporary surveillance is rhizomatic, that it is like a plant that grows in surface extensions through interconnected vertical root systems. The rhizome lacks a centralized structure like a trunk, and so does contemporary surveillance. Surveillance technologies are undertaken by diverse agencies and organizations and therefore operate by variation and disjunction. Like offshoots the rhizome throws in different places, contemporary surveillance grows by expanding its uses in different realms, by targeting new populations, such as students, caregivers, employees, commuters, travelers, and tenants.

Ericson and Haggerty also use the rhizome metaphor to show that contemporary surveillance has a leveling effect on hierarchies, which goes against the model offered by Orwell (1949) and Foucault. Unlike top-down surveillance where a few powerful individuals or groups watch the many, surveillance in contemporary society "has transformed hierarchies of observation, and allows for the scrutiny of the powerful by both institutions and the general population" (Ericson and Haggerty, 617). For example, the poor come into contact with social assistance or the criminal justice system, and become targets of surveillance. Meanwhile, the middle and upper classes come into contact with a greater number of institutions, and are thus subject to more scrutiny in terms of their consumption habits, communication patterns, financial transactions, Internet use, credit history, transportation patterns, health profile, etc.

In addition, people can scrutinize their leaders through mass media. Television in particular enables the many to focus on, observe and monitor the few. Handheld cameras help people to tape instances of police brutality and thus level the hierarchy of surveillance. Cumulatively, these various developments point to a "fractured criss-crossing of the gaze such that no major population groups stand irrefutably above or outside of the surveillant assemblage" (618).

Multi-directional or criss-crossing nature of contemporary surveillance is also discussed by Lyon (1994), who notes that in contemporary surveillance systems power does not flow through a single channel, and that the inherent power found in surveillance systems is not exercised by the state only. Increasingly, non-governmental entities, most prominently private corporations (banks, credit card companies, HMO's, etc.) are extending the surveillance apparatus, changing the parameters of power in the information age, and diminishing relevance of the Orwellian model of centralized state power.

In a similar vein, Staples (2000) describes surveillance practices in contemporary society as "bi-directional," in that they do not simply operate from top-down, but circulate throughout the social body. Unlike an Orwellian nightmare, bi-directional surveillance does not imply a simplistic flow of power; it is dispersed. Contemporary surveillance practices are no longer the exclusive birth right of the few; rather they are practiced by a wide range of social actors. For example, parents use hidden cameras to check on their babysitters; local police departments resort to cameras at traffic lights; employers monitor workers' computer files, e-mails, Internet usage, phone conversations, etc. (26). Whitaker (1999) also directs our attention to the growth of the "informal exercise of power outside the state structure," and asserts that totalitarian visions of power are mistaken since we are experiencing a "transition from the surveillance state to the surveillance society" (29).

These conceptualizations do throw light on new modes of video surveillance. As I mentioned in the Introduction, video surveillance programs are not deployed by social institutions only (although in this study I have focused on such programs); indeed non-institutional applications have permeated daily life in diverse public and private spaces.

As Haggerty (2006) notes, these non-institutional programs deployed by private entities do not simply serve a single coherent purpose such as social control, but a plethora of projects, including deterrence, consumption, entertainment, child-rearing, health promotion (28). It would be revealing to explore the intensification of video surveillance, its perception and implications in workplaces, retail stores, restaurants, daycare centers, etc. Such a project would not only enable us to explore different power dynamics at work, but would show points of convergence and divergence between video surveillance programs in a wide array of social spaces.

Another insightful conceptualization of contemporary surveillance is offered by Thomas Mathiesen (1997) who revisits the Foucaldian panoptic paradigm and argues contemporary surveillance must be understood in relation to mass media. Mathiesen argues that mass media, specifically television enables large numbers of people focusing on something in common, reversing the Panoptic model of the few watching the many:

> The mass media, and especially television today bring the many—literally hundreds of millions of people at the same time—with great force to see and admire the few. In contrast to Foucault's panoptical process, the latter process is referred to as synoptical (215).

While the panoptic paradigm enables the few to observe the many through a hierarchical system, the synoptic paradigm allows just the opposite: the many can see "the few - the VIPs, the reporters, the stars, almost a new class in the public sphere" (219). Although synoptical observation is conceptualized as an opposing force, Mathiesen claims that it does more than to simply enable the many to focus on something common. Synoptic observation works in tandem or is fused with the panoptical supervision; it is intimately tied to the impulse of panoptic supervision, that is, visibility as a desirable aim.

Focusing on the role of mass media in synopticism, Mathiesen explains that mass media not only shapes our understandings of surveillance, but also promotes visibility. It is the fusion of panoptic and synoptic mechanisms that helps to achieve control in the surveillant regime today. Sean Hier (2007) uses the example of the mediation of September 11 terrorist attacks to clarify this fusion:

> Repeated exposure to graphic visual imagery of the attacks served to invite a global audience to consume the hybrid image of fascination and repulsion whilst those same images served as, and remain, the central discursive resource oriented towards consolidating panoptical aspirations through the intensification of information gathering, data sharing and risk management techniques (122).

To this I would add the video footage of Columbine school shootings as a media moment whereby synoptic and panoptic dynamics worked in tandem to foster visibility and reinforce the surveillant regime. While television audiences watched the surveillance footage of this horrific crime, they not only focused on something common, but more significantly they participated in media and law enforcement discourse supporting surveillance systems in schools and elsewhere to prevent future tragedies.

Another point of departure from the Panoptic model of video surveillance has to do with the implied power positions the watchers occupy. Although in this study I have not been able to interview police officers, I am nonetheless compelled to question the empowered position of the watchers. As I discussed in Chapter 4, some administrators and teachers, who are aware of their own visibility, said they feel the fear of being caught on tape themselves. In light of these narratives, we should be cautious about drawing conclusions about the watchers as empowered individuals, and instead explore their experiences to reveal possible contradictions or ambiguities.

Along these lines, Smith's (2009) ethnographic research is particularly insightful. Smith questions the depiction of operators as empowered, God-like disciplinary agents, and argues that the watchers' power within the CCTV system is nothing but ambiguous. Through interviews with CCTV operators, Smith documents how these agents experience powerlessness because of their lack of operational freedom, their position at the bottom of a social control hierarchy, their inability intervene in the physical action being watched and the erosion of their anonymity by court appearances (133-140).

Notions of Privacy

The second research question in this study is concerned with conceptualizations of privacy. How do individuals make sense of privacy and private space? To answer this and other related questions, I have focused on individuals who are objects of video surveillance in Washington Square Park and the schools, and probed how they discuss the outcomes of video surveillance for privacy and express their concerns—if any—about cameras and privacy invasion.

Typically, it is argued that video surveillance leads to privacy invasion and that people find this disconcerting. However, as I noted in Chapter 4, most students and park visitors do not see surveillance cameras as bothersome or as invasive in terms of privacy. This is primarily because they view video surveillance as a safety tool that works in the public interest.

In schools for example, students are aware of the shortcomings of the surveillance system but they nevertheless consider it as helpful in ensuring safety and discipline. In Washington Square Park, park visitors made similar arguments in regard to public safety and clearing out of drug dealers or other unsavory characters from the park, and argued that public interest prevails over individual privacy concerns. In short, the perceived benefits of video surveillance and the prevalence of public safety discourse over individual privacy lead park visitors and students to shun negative feelings about video surveillance.

Further, individuals generally associate expectation of privacy in public settings with some sort of wrongdoing. They reason, if a person wants to enjoy privacy in a public setting then he/she must be craving secrecy or must be doing something wrong. This is because privacy is usually associated with secrecy, isolation or the personal realm. It is generally argued that privacy exists in the home, and being seen, watched or observed—be it by passersby or the police—is part and parcel of public life.

Although most students and park visitors I interviewed said they are not worried about privacy, there were exceptions to this generalization. For example, some female park users in Washington Square Park said they are particularly troubled by the possibility of male police officers using the cameras to leer at them. African-American men remarked that they believed to be disproportionately targeted by surveillance cameras because of their skin color.

In a similar vein, African-American students at Jefferson High School said they were not concerned by the cameras in their school but by cameras in retail environments because they thought they were perceived as shoplifters because of their skin color. These findings show that the outcomes of video surveillance are experienced differently by different people in different contexts. Expectations of and desires for privacy vary along the axes of race, gender, socio-economic status, and most importantly according to the public setting and the watchers in question.

Directions for Future Research

Surveillance and Citizen Mobilization after September 11

The intensification of surveillance after September 11 and the implementation of various homeland security efforts that reinforce the overall surveillance regime also constitute a worthwhile topic to investigate. For example, some key developments that took place after September 11 deserve attention to examine the larger socio-political context of surveillance, first and foremost the PATRIOT Act and the expansion of surveillance through legislative initiatives; plans to introduce CAPSS (Computer Assisted Passenger Pre-Screening System) to conduct background checks on all airline passengers by collecting information about their financial and transactional data; the launching of the U.S.-VISIT program (U.S. Visitor and Immigrant Status Indicator Technology) to verify the identity of foreign visitors through biometric technology; introduction of the SEVIS program (Student Exchange and Visitor Information System) to track and collect information about foreign students and scholars.

Against the backdrop of these anti-terrorism measures, leading scholars in surveillance studies have examined key surveillance programs introduced after September 11.[5] However, we need further studies that investigate the public support these surveillance program garner, with the primary focus on the public perception of surveillance and the understanding of the social, cultural dynamics behind this phenomenon.

For example, in the aftermath of September 11, as various polls have shown, public opinion gave broad support to surveillance activities especially in the context of anti-terrorism and homeland security efforts. According to a Harris poll of September 2001, 86% of respondents favored the use of facial recognition technology in public spaces, 81% supported closer monitoring of bank and credit card records, 68% were in favor of a national ID card, and 63% approved expansion of camera surveillance ("Privacy in an age of terror," p. 86). In 2002, a Search poll found that the majority of the public (84-88%) thought it was acceptable for the government to use biometric surveillance as part of its anti-terrorism campaign. 82% of those surveyed thought it likely that "our society will adopt [privacy] safeguards if and when biometric surveillance is widely used." Another 62% said the government would use biometrics for anti-terrorism investigations and "not misuse [it] in ways that would threaten legitimate privacy" ("Government uses of biometrics," pp. 7, 9).

At this point, it is important to acknowledge the particular instances of "resistance" to increased surveillance. Privacy advocacy and civil liberties groups, first and foremost Electronic Privacy Information Center and American Civil Liberties Union, adamantly opposed the new anti-terrorism legislation and the increasing use of surveillance technologies. Meanwhile, more than 330 communities and 4 states (Alaska, Hawaii, Maine, and Vermont) criticized or expressed concern about the PATRIOT Act (Egan, 2004); the American Library Association decried the turning over of library records to federal agents; the City Council of Washington, DC held public hearings on the surveillance camera network and asked the DC police to draft legislation regarding the use of cameras. In late 2005 when news of secret government monitoring of phone conversations broke, public opinion reacted against such intrusions, and Bush administration was criticized of domestic spying. [6] At the time, a CBS News poll showed that 59% of respondents rejected the idea of government agencies regularly monitoring their phone calls and were dissatisfied with government's handling of civil liberties (Angus Reid, 2006).

Yet as other polls indicate, despite concerns about privacy and civil liberties, the majority of public opinion continues to endorse surveillance efforts. For example, in 2003, a Harris poll showed that most Americans (67-77%) approved the use of facial recognition technology at various locations and public events, expanded camera surveillance on streets and in public places, and closer monitoring of banking and credit card transactions (Harris Poll 2003). Although the majority of respondents in a CNN/USA Today/Gallup poll said the government's actions in the war on terror should not violate civil liberties, an even larger majority felt the Bush administration had not done so, and they were not worried about any encroachment (Gallup Poll 2003). In a 2004 Harris poll, only 14% of the respondents said the government's anti-terrorism program violated their privacy, while the majority endorsed the strict measures taken to prevent terrorism (Harris Poll 2004). According to a 2006 ABC News/Washington Post poll, Americans divided about evenly on the specific issue of warrantless wiretaps by the National Security Agency: 51% called them acceptable in investigating terrorism, 47% unacceptable. The same poll also found that, those who called privacy a greater concern have increased from 21% in 2003 to 32%, while still heavily outnumbered by those who did not (ABC News 2006).

Aside from the public support given to video surveillance and other anti-terrorism measures, we should also pay attention to post-September 11 citizen mobilization efforts. For example, in 2002, President Bush called upon Americans to get involved in strengthening their communities, and "foster a culture of responsibility, service, and citizenship." Meanwhile, Attorney General John Ashcroft announced a plan to incorporate terrorism prevention into the existing crime prevention mission of the Neighborhood Watch program ("Neighborhood Watch Gets Residents Prepared"). The Department of Homeland Security, on the other hand, kicked off its Ready campaign whereby it advised citizens to prepare an emergency plan for their families, assemble a home emergency kit, and be informed about biological, nuclear, and chemical attacks (Hay and Andrejevic 2006).

These and similar appeals to the public to play an active role in the war on terror constitute an important dimension of homeland security efforts. One of the most mundane illustrations of this phenomenon is the simple yet potent message, which has become ubiquitous at New York City subway stations and trains. It reads, "If you see something, say something."

As fear of terrorism becomes the dominant cultural theme, and public safety turns into the perennial concern of not just the government but of everyone, citizens are invited to support surveillance as well as to enter into both real and symbolic partnerships with law enforcement. In this process, public authorities encourage citizens to be rational, cautious, and crime-conscious, and throw upon them the responsibility for risk management. Working together with the police, citizens watch their surroundings for suspicious activity, become the "eyes and ears" of the law enforcement, and participate in the war on terror and the surveillance apparatus it deploys.

Sousveillance

Ordinary citizens increasingly engage in surveillance technologies and practices. From parents who use nannycams to watch their babysitters to neighborhood watch groups who keep an eye on unfamiliar persons on their block, contemporary surveillance extends its reach beyond institutional boundaries. This phenomenon is generally referred to as peer-to-peer or lateral surveillance, that is ordinary individuals monitoring other ordinary individuals. To this, we can also add the phenomenon of sousveillance, which refers to surveillance of authority figures by watchful citizens, such as those who use handicams to expose police brutality (Mann 2004).[7] While lateral surveillance or peer monitoring refers to individuals gathering information about friends, family members, love interests, employees, etc., sousveillance is specifically about visual surveillance.[8]

In this study, my focus has been on sur-veillance—watching from above. Yet contemporary surveillance is increasingly fused with sous-veillance, which warrants an investigation of how handicams and camera phone organize/reorganize visual documentation in digital culture by enabling ordinary citizens to engage in observation and control. Unlike top-down surveillance where a few powerful individuals or groups watch the many, sousveillance has "transformed hierarchies of observation [allowing] for the scrutiny of the powerful by both institutions and the general population" (Ericson and Haggerty 2000, 617).

These new formations of surveillance are non-systematic, non-continuous, and carried out by citizens. Therefore, they fall outside the theoretical model of the Panopticon. They rely on the use of handicams and cell phone cameras, not surveillance cameras, to produce video footage of "real" events (e.g. police beatings caught on tape). They also involve the use of video-sharing websites which allow fast and easy distribution and consumption of video footage.

Handicams and cell phone cameras are generally conceptualized as instruments that we can believe in as neutral recorders of truth and reality. They stand as symbols of neutral vision and transparency mostly because they serve as "nonhuman witnesses" in the sense that human capacities are irrelevant to their operation. As such, these technologies have begun to occupy a central position within the matrix of visual documentation and the construction of truth and reality.[9] In addition, it is generally believed that users embrace handicams and cell phone cameras as emancipatory tools to produce and distribute their own content and eventually to intervene in or puncture the discourse of authorities. As user-generated content online and on television has become more prevalent and popular, these technologies are generally considered as instruments of activism, emancipation, intervention or meaningful media participation. Some questions to discuss in detail are: In what ways do specific uses of handicams, cell phone cameras and video-sharing websites mark the emergence of a decentralized system where citizens can now share the power to observe and control? And if this decentralized system is one where these visual technologies are players in a complex network of surveillance/sousveillance, how can we conceptualize them—as tools that empower citizens or make them implicit partners in the surveillance infrastructure? How can we best address the reconfiguration of the relationship between producers and consumers of visual imagery, the changing nature of surveillance society by way of citizen-produced "caught on tape" videos, and the intensification of visibility?

In answering these questions, we must evaluate handicams and camera phones as key players in the surveillance /sousveillance culture. While the photographic/video camera is aligned with the closed and static structure of the Panopticon, surveillance /sousveillance powers of handicams and cell phone cameras offer glimpses into the more complex, decentralized networks of the synoptic paradigm. Cell phone cameras intensify the visibility of anyone, anytime, anywhere as they aid in the proliferation of lateral surveillance as well as sousveillance. With the disappearance of the definite existence of the camera and the disembodiment of the corporeal observer, they dramatically transform the public and the private, the observer and the observed.

In thinking of the roles handicams and cell phone cameras play in these cultural developments, we also need to keep in mind that these visual communication technologies work together with the broadcasting powers of the Internet in creating a new mode of visual documentation and communication. Images captured on handicams and cell phone cameras in the style of "caught-on-tape" footage are not simply intended for personal viewing, but to be circulated and made public. Therefore, we also need to address the changing patterns of production/consumption of visual imagery in the contemporary surveillance/sousveillance culture by paying specific attention to the Internet, which acts as an outlet for users to share their recordings and make them public.

Notes

[1] The turn to crime prevention did not (and does not) suggest that the courts and law enforcement entirely abandon incarceration in favor of preventive strategies. There are and always will be offenders who need to be apprehended and/or punished for the violations they commit. The aim of crime prevention is not to do away with incarceration or to *eliminate* crime, but to *reduce* crime in the first place by deterring people. Another point to be considered is that crime prevention and the attendant risk management approaches significantly broaden the definition of crime, and target a wide array of behaviors that range from criminal acts to minor offenses or disruptive acts. It can be argued that crime prevention is not merely a program of crime reduction, but also a project of general control and administration of daily life. In the schools, for example, video surveillance—a preventive apparatus—targets not only criminal acts (assault, murder, etc) but "unruly" or "disorderly" behavior (cutting class) and extends the watchful eye of the authorities to a wide range of behaviors.

[2] See http://www.mediaeater.com/cameras/info/cb-02.html and http://www.appliedautonomy.com/isee.html

[3] I have also discussed this in Yesil, Bilge. 2006. "Watching Ourselves: Video Surveillance, Urban Space and Self-Responsibilization." *Cultural Studies*. 20: 4-5, 400-416.

[4] For a detailed discussion see Yesil, 2006.

[5] For a detailed discussion, see Lyon, 2003; Lyon, 2006; Whitaker, 2006, Zureik and Salter, 2006; Adey, 2006; Van Der Ploeg, 2006; Webb, 2007; Jones, 2009

[6]See Risen James and Eric Lichtblau. 2005. "Bush Lets U.S. Spy on Callers without Courts." *The New York Times.* December 16, Leslie Cauley and John Diamond. 2006. "Telecoms Let NSA Spy on Calls." *USA Today.* February 6.

[7] For a detailed discussion, see Mann Steve, Jason Nolan and Barry Wellman. 2003. "Sousveillance: Inventing and Using Wearable Computing Devices for Data Collection in Surveillance Environments" *Surveillance & Society* 1(3): 331-355. http://www.surveillance-and-society.org

[8] For a detailed discussion of lateral surveillance, see Andrejevic, Mark. 2005. "The Work of Watching One Another: Lateral Surveillance, Risk, and Governance." *Surveillance and Society.* 2(4): 479-497. http://surveillance-and-society.org

[9] The problematic relationship between image and truth is perhaps best illustrated by dueling videos—shot by civilians and the police—of 2009 student protests at the New School. See Halbfinger, David M. 2009. "At New School protest, truth depends on camera angle. *The New York Times.* April 12.

References

Aas Katja Franko, Oppen Gundhus Helene and Heidi Mork Lomell (eds). 2008. *Technologies of Insecurity: The Surveillance of Everyday Life.* New York: Routledge-Cavendish.

ABC News/Washington Post Poll. 2006. "Broader Concern on Privacy Rights, but Terrorism Threat Still Trumps." January 10, http:// abcnews .go.com/Politics/story?id=1490715.

American Civil Liberties Union. 2008. *What Criminologists and Others Studying Cameras have found.* June 25, http: //www.aclu.org /images/asset_upload_file708_35775.pdf.

Angus Reid Global Monitor. 2006. "Americans Reject Phone, Email Surveillance." September 10. http://www.angus-reid.com /polls /view /13091.

Adey, Peter. 2006. "Divided we Move? The Dromologics of Airport Security and Surveillance." In *Surveillance and Security: Technological Politics and Power in Everyday Life*, edited by Torin Monahan, 195-208. New York: Routledge.

Agre, Philip, and Marc Rotenberg. 1998. *Technology and Privacy: The New Landscape.* Cambridge, MA: MIT Press.

Agre, Philip. 2001. "Your Face is not a Barcode: Arguments against Automatic Face Recognition in Public Places." *Whole Earth.* Winter: 74-77.

Allen, Anita. 1999. "Coercing Privacy." *William and Mary Law Review*. 40 (3): 723-762.

Alvesson, Mats, and Kaj Skoldberg. 2000. *Reflexive Methodology: New Vistas for Qualitative Research.* London: Sage.

"A mom's 'bad day' turns into TV spectacle. 2002. *Buffalo News*. September 24.

Andrejevic, Mark. 2007. *I-Spy: Surveillance and Power in the Interactive Era.* University Press of Kansas.

Archibold, Randal. 1998. "Schools in Deal to Let Police Run Security." *The New York Times*. August 29.

Archibold, Randal. 1998. "New Era as Police Prepare to Run School Security. *The New York Times.* September 16.

Barnabel, Josh. 1993. "Improvements in School Security Force Proposed." *The New York Times.* April 9.

Barry, Andrew, Thomas Osborne and Nikolas Rose (eds). 1996. *Foucault and Political Reason: Liberalism, Neo-liberalism, and Rationalities of Government.* Chicago: University of Chicago Press.

Beck, Ulrich. 1992. *Risk Society: Toward a New Modernity.* London: Sage.

Bennett, Colin. 2008. *The Privacy Advocates: Resisting the Spread of Surveillance.* Cambridge, MA: MIT Press.

Bennett, Colin and Rebecca Grant. 1999. *Visions of Privacy: Policy Choices for the Digital Age.* Toronto: University of Toronto Press.

Bentham, Jeremy. 1781. *An Introduction to the Principles of Morals and Legislation.* London: E. Wilson.

Block, Robert. 2007. "U.S. to Expand Domestic Use of Spy Satellites." *The Wall Street Journal.* August 16. http://online.wsj.com /public /article /SB118714764716998275.html

Bloustein, Edward. 1984. "Privacy as an Aspect of Human Dignity." In *Philosophical Dimensions of Privacy: An Anthology*, edited by Ferdinand Schoeman, 156-202. Cambridge, UK: Cambridge University Press.

Boddy, Trevor. 1992. "Underground and Overhead: Building the Analogous City." In *Variations on a Theme Park: The New American City and the End of Public Space*, 123-153. New York: Hill and Wang.

Bowyer, Kevin. 2004. "Face Recognition Technology: Security versus Privacy." *IEEE Technology and Society Magazine* 23. http ://www .patmedia.net/tbookman/techsoc/bowyer.html

Bozovic, Miran. 1995. *The Panopticon Writings: Jeremy Bentham.* New York: Verso.

Bravin, Jeremy. 2002. "Washington Police to Play 'I Spy.' *The Wall Street Journal.* February 13.

Brey, Philip. 2004. "Ethical Aspects of Facial Recognition Systems in Public Places." In *Readings in Cyberethics*, edited by Richard Tavani and Herbert Spinello, 457-479. Boston: Jones and Bartlett Publishers.

Brin, David. 1999. *The Transparent Society: Will Technology Force Us to Choose Between Privacy and Freedom?* Basic Books.

Brown, Sheila. 1998. "What's the Problem, Girls? CCTV and the Gendering of Public Safety." In *Surveillance, Closed Circuit Television and Social Control,* edited by Clive Norris, Jade Moran, and Gary Armstrong, 207-220. Aldershot, UK: Ashgate Publishing.

Buckley, Cara. 2007. "Police Plan Web of Surveillance for Downtown." *The New York Times.* July 9.

Burchell, Graham, Colin Gordon, and Peter Miller (eds). 1991. *The Foucault Effect: Studies in Governmentality.* Chicago: University of Chicago Press.

Burge, Kathleen. 2004. "Park Bench in Eye of Wellfleet Storm." *The Boston Globe.* August 30.

Cate, Fred. 1997. *Privacy in the Information Age.* Washington D.C.: Brookings Institution Press.

Carmody, Deirdre. 1988. "Educators Rethink Ways to Make Schools Safe." *The New York Times.* July 27.

Castel, Robert. 1991. "From Dangerousness to Risk." In *The Foucault Effect: Studies in Governmentality*, edited by Graham Burchell, Colin Gordon, and Peter Miller, 281-298. Chicago: The University of Chicago Press.

CBS News. 2002. "Americans OK with Video Scrutiny." April 21. http://www.cbsnews.com/stories/02/04/21/opinion/polls/506822.shtml.

Chan, Sewell. 2005. "New Cameras to Watch over Subway System." *The New York Times.* August 24.

Christopherson, Susan. 1994. "The Fortress City: Privatized Spaces, Consumer Citizenship." In *Post-Fordism: A Reader*, edited by Ash Amin, 409-427. Cambridge, MA: Blackwell.

Chira, Susan. 1982. "A Back to Basics Plan for School Crime." *The New York Times.* December 5.

Clark, Vernon. 2007. "Police Bolster Ability to Monitor the Streets." *The Philadelphia Inquirer.* December 20.

CITRIS (The Center for Information Technology Research in the Interest of Society) 2008. "San Francisco Community Safety Camera Program." December 17. http://www.citris-uc. org/files /CITRIS _SF_CSC_Study_Final_Dec_2008.pdf.

Clarke, Roger. 1997. "Introduction to Dataveillance and Information Privacy, and Definitions of Terms." http://www. anu.edu.au/ people/ Roger.Clarke/DV/Intro.html

Clements, Bill. 2003. "Big Brother's Corporate Sponsor." *City Pages.* June 18. http://www.citypages.com/2003-06-18/news/big-brother-s-corporate-sponsor/

Cohen, Stan. 1979. "The Punitive City: Notes on the Dispersal of Social Control." *Contemporary Crises*. 3: 339-363.

Cohen, Stan. 1985. *Visions of Social Control: Crime, Punishment and Classification.* Cambridge: Polity Press.

Coleman, Roy. 2007. "Surveillance in the City: Primary Definition and Urban Spatial Order." In *The Surveillance Studies Reader,* edited by Sean Hier and Joshua Greenberg, 231-244. Mc Graw-Hill.

Cooper, Michael. 1997. "With Success of Cameras, Concerns over Privacy." *The New York Times*. February 5.

Cranz, Galen. 1982. *The Politics of Park Design: A History of Parks in America*. Cambridge, MA: MIT Press.

Crary, James. 1990. *Techniques of the Observer: On Vision and Modernity in the Nineteenth Century*. Cambridge, MA: The MIT Press.

Culotta, Karen Ann. 2009. "Chicago Links Street Cameras to Its 911 Network." *The New York Times.* February 21.

Danielson, Richard. 1996. "Smile, Ybor: You're on Crime Camera." *St. Petersburg Times*. June 7.

Dandeker, Christopher. 1990. *Surveillance, Power and Modernity: Bureaucracy and Discipline from 1700 to the Present Day*. New York: St. Martin's Press.

Davies, Simon. 1996. *Big brother: Britain's Web of Surveillance and the New Technological Order*. London: Pan.

Davies, Simon. 1998a. "CCTV: A New Battleground for Privacy." In *Surveillance, Closed Circuit Television and Social Control*, edited by Clive Norris, Jade Moran, and Gary Armstrong, 243-254. Aldershot, UK: Ashgate Publishing.

Davies, Simon. 1998b. "Re-engineering the Right to Privacy: How Privacy has been Transformed from a Right to a Commodity." In *Technology and Privacy: The New Landscape*, edited by Philip Agre and Marc Rotenberg. Cambridge, MA: The MIT Press, 1998.

Davis, Mike. 1992. "Fortress Los Angeles: The Militarization of Urban Space." In *Variations on a Theme Park: The New American City and the End of Public Space*, edited by Michael Sorkin, 154-180. New York: Hill and Wang.

Deleuze, Gilles and Felix Guattari. 1987. *A Thousand Plateaus: Capitalism and Schizophrenia.* (B. Massumi, Trans.). Minneapolis: The University of Minnesota Press.

Deleuze, Gilles. 1992. "Postscript on the Societies of Control." *October.* 59: 3-7.

Dennis, Brady. 2003. "Ybor Cameras won't Seek What They Never Found." *St. Petersburg Times*. August 20.

Denzin, Norman and Yvonna S. Lincoln. 1998. "Introduction: Entering the Field of Qualitative Research." In *The Landscape of Qualitative Research,* edited by Norman Denzin and Yvonna S. Lincoln, 1-35. Thousand Oaks: Sage.

Devine, John. 1996. *Maximum Security: The Culture of Violence in Inner-City Schools*. Chicago: University of Chicago Press.

Dillon, Sam. 1993. "On the Barricades Against Violence in the Schools," *The New York Times.* December 24.

Dillon, Sam. 2003. "Cameras Watching Students." *The New York Times.* September 24.

Dority, Barbara. 1997. "Big Brother Goes to High School." *The Humanist.* 57: 38.

Doyle, Aaron. 2006. "An Alternative Current in Surveillance and Control: Broadcasting Surveillance Footage of Crimes." In *The New Politics of Surveillance and Visibility,* edited by Kevin D. Haggerty and Richard V. Ericson. 199-224. Toronto: University of Toronto Press.

Doyle, Charles. 1992. *Wiretapping and Electronic Surveillance: The Electronic Communications Privacy Act and Related Matters.* Washington D.C.: Congressional Research Service, Library of Congress.

Dunlap, David. 2008. "Unblinking Eyes for $20 million, at Freedom Tower." *The New York Times.* September 24.

Egan, Timothy. 2004. "Sensing the Eyes of Big Brother, and Pushing Back." *The New York Times.* August 8.

EPIC (Electronic Privacy Information Center) (n.d.) "Face Recognition." http://epic.org/privacy/facerecognition.

Ellin, Nan. 1997. "Shelter from the Storm or Form Follows Fear and Vice Versa." In *Architecture of Fear,* edited by Nan Ellin, 13-31. New York: Princeton Architectural Press.

Ellul, Jacques. 1964. *The Technological Society.* (J. Wilkinson, Trans.). New York: Knopf.

Ericson, Richard V. and Kevin D. Haggerty. 1997. *Policing the Risk Society.* Toronto: The University of Toronto Press.

Ericson Richard V. and Kevin D. Haggerty. 2000. "The Surveillant Assemblage." *British Journal of Sociology.* 51 (4): 605-622.

Ericson Richard V. and Kevin D. Haggerty. (eds.) 2006. *The New Politics of Surveillance and Visibility.* Toronto: University of Toronto Press.

Etzioni, Amitai. 1999. *The Limits of Privacy.* New York: Basic Books.

Feely, Malcolm and Jonathan Simon. 1994. "Actuarial Justice: The Emerging New Criminal Law." In *The Futures of Criminology*, edited by David Nelken, 173-201. London: Sage.

Fiske, John. 2000. "Videotech." In *The Visual Culture Reader*, edited by Nick Mirzoeff, 153-162. New York; Routledge.

Flusty, Steven. 1997. "Building Paranoia." In *Architecture of Fear,* edited by Nan Ellin, 47-60. New York: Princeton Architectural Press.

Fortner, Robert. 1986. "Physics and Metaphysics in an Information Age: Privacy, Dignity and Identity." *Communication.* 9: 151-172.

Foucault, Michel. 1980. "Prison Talk." In *Power/Knowledge: Selected Interviews and Other Writings, 1972-1977,* edited by Colin Gordon, 37-54. New York: Pantheon.

Foucault, Michel. 1977. *Discipline and Punish: The Birth of the Prison.* New York: Vintage Books.

Foucault, Michel. 1983. "Afterword: The Subject and Power." In *Michel Foucault: Beyond Structuralism and Hermeneutics,* edited by Richard Dreyfus and Paul Rabinow, 208-226. Chicago: The University of Chicago Press.

Foucault, Michel. 1991. "Governmentality." In *The Foucault Effect: Studies in Governmentality,* edited by Graham Burchell, Colin Gordon, and Paul Miller, 87-104. Chicago: The University of Chicago Press.

Freedman, Warren. 1987. *The Right of Privacy in the Computer Age.* New York: Quorum Books.

Fyfe, Nicholas and John Bannister. 1998. "The Eyes upon the Street: Closed-Circuit Television Surveillance and the City." In *Images of the Street: Planning, Identity and Control in Public Space,* edited by Nicholas Fyfe, 248-260. London and New York: Routledge.

Gallup Poll. 2003. "Public Little Concerned About Patriot Act." September 9. http://www.gallup.com/ content/login.aspx?ci=9205.

Gandy, Oscar. 1989. "The Surveillance Society: Information Technology and Bureaucratic Social Control." *Journal of Communication.* 39 (3): 61-76.

Gandy, Oscar. 1993. *The Panoptic Sort: A Political Economy of Personal Information.* Boulder: Westview Press.

Garfinkel, Simon. 2000. *Database Nation :The Death of Privacy in the 21st Century.* Cambridge, UK : O'Reilly.

Garland, David. 1996. "The Limits of the Sovereign State: Strategies of Crime Control in Contemporary Society." *The British Journal of Criminology.* 36(4): 445 –471.

Garland, David. 2001. *The Culture of Control: Crime and Social Order in Contemporary Society.* Chicago: University of Chicago Press.

Garrison, John. 2004. "Cameras to Keep Watch in Hollywood." *The Los Angeles Times.* October 28.

Gates, Kelly. 2006. "Identifying the 9/11 'Faces of Terror': The Promise and Problem of Facial Recognition Technology." *Cultural Studies* 20 (4/5): 417-440.

Gavison, Ruth. 1980. "Privacy and the Limits of Law." *The Yale Law Journal.* 89 (3): 421-471.

General Accounting Office. 2003. *Report 03-748: Video Surveillance: Information on Law Enforcement's Use of Closed-Circuit Television to Monitor Selected Federal Property in Washington, D.C.*

Gergen, Kenneth. 1999. *An Invitation to Social Construction.* Thousand Oaks, CA: Sage.

Gettleman, Jeffrey. 1998. "Cameras Keep Eye on Ybor Masses." *St. Petersburg Times.* September 6.

Giddens, Anthony. 1991. *Modernity and Self-Identity: Self and Society in the Late Modern Age.* Stanford, CA: Stanford University Press.

Gilliom, John. 1996. *Surveillance, Privacy, and the Law : Employee Drug Testing and the Politics of Social Control.* Ann Arbor, MI: The University of Michigan Press.

Gilliom, John. 2001. *Overseers of the Poor: Surveillance, Resistance, and the Limits of Privacy.* Chicago: The University of Chicago Press.

Ginsberg, Allan. 2002. "Schools to Get Cams." *The Daily News.* November 4.

Goldman, Ari. 1983. "Crime in Subway Station Rises in spite of TV Monitors." *The New York Times.* February 5.

Goodnough, Abby. 1998. "Mayor Defends Growth of Video Surveillance." *The New York Times*. December 14.

Goold, Benjamin. 2004. *CCTV and Policing: Public Area Surveillance and Police Practices in Britain.* Oxford: Oxford University Press.

"Government Uses of Biometrics." 2002. *Privacy and American Business.* 9(8): 7-9.

Graham, Stephen. 1998. "Towards the Fifth Utility? On the Extension and Normalization of Public CCTV." In *Surveillance, Closed Circuit Television and Social Control,* edited by Clive Norris, Jade Moran, and Gary Armstrong, 89-112. Aldershot, England: Ashgate Publishing.

Guba, Egon G. and Yvonna S. Lincoln. 1989. *Fourth Generation Evaluation.* Newbury Park, CA: Sage.

Guba, Egon G. and Yvonna S. Lincoln. 1998. "Competing Paradigms in Qualitative Research." In *The Landscape of Qualitative Research: Theories and Issues,* edited by Norman Denzin and Yvonna S. Lincoln, 195-220. Thousand Oaks: Sage.

Gramsci, Antonio. 1971. *Selections from the Prison Notebooks of Antonio Gramsci.* (Quentin Hoare and Geoffrey Nowell Smith, Trans.) New York: International Publishers.

Grunwald, Michael. 1996. "Guards and Cameras Cut Crime in Three Projects." *The Boston Globe.* May 8.

Haggerty, Kevin D. 2006. "Tear Down the Walls: On Demolishing the Panopticon." In *Theorizing Surveillance: Panopticon and Beyond*, edited by David Lyon. Devon, UK: Willan Publishing.

Hafner, Katie. 2003. "Where the Hall Monitor is a Webcam." *The New York Times.* February 27.

Hay, Colin. 1996. "Mobilization through Interpellation: James Bulger, Juvenile Crime and the Construction of a Moral Panic." *Social and Legal Studies.* 4: 197-223.

Hay, James. 2003. "Unaided Virtues: The (Neo)-liberalization of the Domestic Sphere and the New Architecture of Community." In *Foucault, Cultural Studies and Governmentality,* edited by Jack Z. Bratich, Jeremy Packer, and Cameron McCarthy, 165-206. Albany. NY: State University of New York Press.

Hay, James and Mark Andrejevic. 2006. "Introduction: Homeland (In)Securities." *Cultural Studies*. 20(4/5): 331-348.

Harris Poll. 2003. "Homeland Security: American Public Continues to Endorse a Broad Range of Proposals for Stronger Surveillance

Powers." March 10. http://www.harrisinteractive.com /harris_poll /index.asp?PID=362.

Harris Poll. 2004. "Strong and Continuing Support for Tough Measures to Prevent Terrorism." March 5. http://www.harrisinteractive .com/harris _poll /index.asp?PID=446.

Hier, Sean and Joshua Greenberg (eds). 2007. *The Surveillance Studies Reader*. McGraw-Hill.

Hoffman, Lisa. 2006. "Under Surveillance: Government Spy Cameras Proliferate in Public Spaces." *Scripps Howard News Service*. June 22. http://www.shns.com/shns/g_index2.cfm?action =detail&pk =SURVEILLANCE-06-22-06

Holloway, Lynette. 1998. "Board Votes to Give Police Control over School Security." *The New York Times*. September 17.

Holtzman, David. 2006. *Privacy Lost: How Technology is Endangering Your Privacy*. John Wiley and Sons.

Hsu, Stephen. 2002. "DC Forms Network of Surveillance." *The Washington Post*. February 17.

International Association of Chiefs of Police. 2001. "Executive Brief: The Use of CCTV/ Video Cameras in Law Enforcement." http://www.theiacp.org/Portals/0/pdfs/Publications/UseofCCTV.pd f

Jacoby, Mary. 2002. "On Patrol for the Terrorist Next Door." *St. Petersburg Times*. 2002, April 8.

Jacobs, Jane. 1961. *The Death and Life of Great American Cities*. New York: Random House.

Jeffery, C. R. 1971. *Crime Prevention through Environmental Design*. Beverly Hills, CA: Sage Publications.

Jensen Derrick and George Draffan. 2004. *Welcome to the Machine: Science, Surveillance, and the Culture of Control*. Chelsea Green.

Jones, Richard. 2008. "Checkpoint Security: Gateways, Airports, and the Architecture of Security." In *Technologies of Insecurity: The Surveillance of Everyday Life*, edited by Katja Franko Aas, Helene Oppen Gundhus and Heidi Mork Lomell, 81-102. New York: Routledge-Cavendish.

Kennedy, Randy. 1997. "Police Cameras Planned for More Housing Projects." *The New York Times*. November 13.

Kilgannon, Corey. 2002. "Cameras to Seek Faces of Terror in Visitors to the Statute of Liberty." *The New York Times*. May 25.

Kincheloe, Joe L. and Peter McLaren. 1998. "Rethinking Critical Theory and Qualitative Research." In *The Landscape of Qualitative Research: Theories and Issues,* edited by Norman Denzin and Yvonna S. Lincoln, 260-289. Thousand Oaks: Sage.

Kinzer, Stephen. 2004. "Chicago Moving to Smart Surveillance Cameras." *The New York Times.* September 21.

Klosek, Jacqueline. 2006. *The War on Privacy.* Praeger.

Knepper Paul and Clive Norris. 2009. "Fingerprint and Photograph: Surveillance Technologies in the Manufacture of Suspect Social Identities." In *Urban Crime Prevention, Surveillance and Restorative Justice,* edited by Paul Knepper, Jonathan Doak and Joanna Shapland, 77-100. Boca Raton, FL: CRC Press.

Kocieniewski, David. 1996. "Television Cameras may Survey Public Places." *The New York Times.* October 6.

Krause, Timothy. 2003. "City Unplugs Camera Software." *Tampa Tribune*. August 20.

Kugler, Sara. 1998. "City must Warn of Vid, Group Sez." *The Daily News.* December 14.

Lambert, Bruce. 1998. "Secret Surveillance Cameras Growing in City, Report Says." *The New York Times.* December 13.

Laudon, Kenneth C. 1996. *Dossier Society: Value Choices in the Design of National Information Systems*. Columbia University Press.

Levin, Thomas, Ursula Frohne, and Peter Weibel. (eds.) 2002. *CTRL[SPACE]: Rhetorics of Surveillance from Bentham to Big Brother.* Cambridge, MA: The MIT Press.

Lincoln, Yvonna S. and Egon G. Guba. 1985. *Naturalistic Inquiry.* Beverly Hills, CA: Sage.

Lindlof, Thomas R. 1995. *Qualitative Communication Research Methods.* Thousand Oaks: Sage.

Lingblom, Marie. 2003. "School Cafeteria's Biometrics System Gets Good Grades." *CRN Channelweb Network.* March 28. http://www.crn.com/sections/news/top_news.asp?ArticleID=40811

Linowes, David F. 1989. *Privacy in America: Is Your Private Life in the Public Eye?* Urbana: The University of Illinois Press.

Lofton, Lisa. 2004. "M.P. Schools Go High Tech." *The Sun Herald.* March 8. http:// www.sunherald.com /mld/sunherald /news/local /8131952.htm.

Lyon, David. 1994. *The Electronic Eye: The Rise of Surveillance Society.* Cambridge, UK: Polity Press, 1994.

Lyon, David and Elia Zureik. 1996. *Computers, Surveillance and Privacy.* Minneapolis: University of Minnesota Press.

Lyon, David. 2001. *Surveillance Society: Monitoring Everyday Life.* Buckhingham, UK: Open University Press, 2001.

Lyon, David. 2003. *Surveillance after September 11*. Cambridge, UK : Polity Press.

Lyon, David. (ed.) 2006. *Theorizing Surveillance: The Panopticon and Beyond.* Portland, OR: Willan Publishing.

Lyon, David. 2007. *Surveillance Studies: An Overview*. Malden, MA: Polity Press.

Maeroff, Gene. 1982. "Students' Crimes against Teachers are down by 22%." *The New York Times.* August 5.

Maeroff, Gene. 1984. "Urban School Officials Say Storing Measures to Curb Violence are Working," *The New York Times.* March 12.

Mann, Steve. 2004. "Sousveillance: Inverse Surveillance in Multimedia Imaging." *Proceedings of the 12th Annual ACM International Conference*. October 10-14.

Marcuse, Herbert. 1998. "The New German Mentality." In *Technology, War and Fascism: Collected Papers of Herbert Marcuse*, edited by Douglas Kellner, 139-174. London: Routledge.

Marshall, Catherine and Gretchen Rossman. 1989. *Designing Qualitative Research*. Newbury Park, CA : Sage.

Marx, Gary T. 1988. *Undercover: Police Surveillance in America.* Berkeley: University of California Press.

McCahill, Mike. 2002. *The Surveillance Web: The Rise of Visual Surveillance in an English City.* Devon, UK: Willan Publishing.

McGrath, John E. 2004. *Loving Big Brother: Performance, Privacy and Surveillance Space.* New York: Routledge.

Means Coleman, Robin. 2000. *African American Viewers and the Black Situation Comedy: Situating Racial Humor.* New York: Garland Publishing.

Metropolitan Police Department. 2002. *Draft General Order on Closed Circuit Television Cameras (Surveillance Cameras).* http://www .dcwatch.com/ police/ 020404.htm

Mills, Jon. 2008. *Privacy: The Lost Right*. Oxford University Press.

Monahan, Torin. 2006. "The Surveillance Curriculum: Risk Management and Social Control in the Neoliberal School." In

Surveillance and Security: Technological Politics and Power in Everyday Life, edited by Torin Monahan, 109-124. New York: Routledge.

Monahan, Torin. (ed.) 2006. *Surveillance and Security: Technological Politics and Power in Everyday Life*. New York: Routledge.

Moore, Benjamin. 1984. *Privacy: Studies in Social and Cultural History.* Armonk, NY: Sharpe.

NACRO. 2002. *To CCTV or Not to CCTV? A Review of Current Research into the Effectiveness of CCTV Systems in Reducing Crime.* http://www.nacro.org.uk/data/resources /nacro2004120299 .pdf

"Neighborhood Watch Gets Residents Prepared." (n.d.) http://www.ridaughtlanding.com/NW/assets/docs/neighborhoodsafety/Neighborhood%20Watch%20Gets%20Residents%20Prepared.pdf

NESRI (National Economic and Social Rights Initiative). 2007. *Deprived of Dignity: Degrading Treatment and Abusive Discipline in New York City and Los Angeles Public Schools.* http://www.nesri.org/programs/Deprived_of_Dignity_07.pdf

Newburn, Tim and Stephanie Hayman. 2001. *Policing, Surveillance and Social Control: CCTV and Police Monitoring of Suspects.* Devon, UK: Willan Publishing.

Newman, Abraham. 2008. *Protectors of Privacy: Regulating Personal Data in the Global Economy.* Ithaca: Cornell University Press.

New York City, Department of Education. "Press Release." 2003. May 3. http://www.nycenet.edu/press/02-03/pr122-03.html

New York City Department of Education. 2005. "School Location Incident Data Report." http://www.nycenet.edu/ourschools/SchoolSafety.htm.

NYCLU (New York Civil Liberties Union). 2006. *Who's Watching? Video Camera Surveillance in New York City and the Need for Public Oversight.* http://www.nyclu.org/pdfs /surveillance_cams_report_121306.pdf

NYCLU. 2007. *Criminalizing the Classroom: The Overpolicing of New York City Schools.* http://www.nyclu.org/files /criminalizing _the_classroom_report.pdf

Nissenbaum, Helen. 1998. "Protecting Privacy in an Information Age: The Problem of Privacy in Public." *Law and Philosophy*. 17: 559-596.

Nissenbaum, Helen. 2004. "Privacy as Contextual Integrity." *Washington Law Review*. 79: 119-158.

Noble, David F. 1999. *The Religion of Technology : The Divinity of Man and the Spirit of Invention*. New York: Knopf.

Norris, Clive and Gary Armstrong. 1999. *The Maximum Surveillance Society: The Rise of CCTV*. Oxford, New York: Berg.

Norris, Clive, Jade Moran, and Gary Armstrong (eds). 1998. *Surveillance, Closed Circuit Television and Social Control*. Aldershot, UK: Ashgate Publishing.

Oakes, Chris. 2000. "Schools Grow Electronic Eyes." *Wired*. August 8. http://www.wired.com/news/culture/0,1284,38082,00.html

O'Hara, Kieron and Nigel Shadbolt.2008. *The Spy in the Coffee Machine: The End of Privacy As We Know It*. Oneworld Publications.

O'Malley, Peter. 1996. "Risk and Responsibility." In *Foucault and Political Reason: Liberalism, Neo-liberalism, and Rationalities of Government*, edited by Andrew Barry, Thomas Osborne, and Nikolas Rose, 189-208. Chicago: The University of Chicago Press.

Orwell, George. 1949. *Nineteen eighty-four*. New York: Harcourt, Brace.

Ouelette, Laurie. 2004. "'Take Responsibility for Yourself': Judge Judy and the Neoliberal Citizen." In *Reality TV: Remaking Television Culture*, edited by Susan Murray and Laurie Ouelette, 231-250. New York: New York University Press.

Parenti, Chris. 2003. *The Soft Cage: Surveillance in America from Slavery to the War on Terror*. New York: Basic Books.

Patton, Michael Quinn. 1990. Qualitative Evaluation and Research Methods. Newbury Park, CA: Sage.

Pennock, Roland and John Chapman. 1971. *Privacy*. New York: Atherton Press.

Postman, Neil. 1993. *Technopoly: The Surrender of Culture to Technology*. New York: Knopf.

"Privacy in an age of terror." 2001. *Business Week*. November 5.

Regan, Priscilla M. 1995. *Legislating Privacy: Technology, Social Values, and Public Policy*. Chapel Hill: The University of North Carolina Press.

Rentschler, Carrie. 2003. "Designing Fear: How Environmental Security Protects Property at the Expense of People." In *Foucault, Cultural Studies, and Governmentality*, edited by Jack Z. Bratich,

Jeremy Packer, and Cameron McCarthy, 243-272. Albany: State University of New York Press.

Rice-Oxley, Mark. 2004. "Big Brother in Britain: Does More Surveillance Work?" *Christian Science Monitor.* February 6. http://www.csmonitor.com/2004/0206/p07s02-woeu.htm.

Roe, Ashley. 2008. "Digital Eyes: The West Palm Beach, Fla., Police Department Increases Officer and Public Safety Using Video Surveillance over Wireless Mesh." *Government Security.* May 1.

Rose, Nikolas. 1996. "Governing 'Advanced' Liberal Democracies." In *Foucault and Political Reason: Liberalism, Neo-liberalism, and Rationalities of Government*, edited by Andrew Barry, Thomas Osborne, and Nikolas Rose, 37-64. Chicago: The University of Chicago Press.

Rosen, Jeffrey. 2001. *The Unwanted Gaze : The Destruction of Privacy in America*. New York : Vintage Books.

Rossler, Beate. 2005. *The Value of Privacy*. Polity Press.

Rule, James B. et al. 1980. *The Politics of Privacy: Planning for Personal Data Systems as Powerful Technologies*. New York: Elsevier.

Rule James B. 2007. *Privacy in Peril: How we are Sacrificing a Fundamental Right in Exchange for Security and Convenience.* Oxford University Press.

Savage, Charlie. 2007. "US Doles out Millions for Street Cameras - Local Efforts Raise Privacy Alarms." *The Boston Globe.* August 12.

Schoeman, Ferdinand. (ed). 1984. *Philosophical Dimensions of Privacy: An Anthology.* Cambridge, UK: Cambridge University Press.

Schwabe, William, Lois Davis, and Brian Jackson. 2001. *Challenges and Choices for Crime-Fighting Technology: Federal Support of State and Local Law Enforcement*. Santa Monica: RAND.

Schwandt, Thomas A. 1998. "Constructivist, Interpretivist Approaches to Human Inquiry." In *The Landscape of Qualitative Research: Theories and Issues,* edited by Norman Denzin and Yvonna S. Lincoln, 221-259. Thousand Oaks: Sage.

Schlosberg, Mark and Nicole Ozer. 2007. *Under the Watchful Eye: The Proliferation of Video Surveillance Systems in California.* http://www.aclunc.org/docs/criminal_justice/police_practices

/under_the_watchful_eye_the_proliferation_of_video_surveillance_systems_in_california.pdf

Schumach, Michael. 1973. "Police to Use TV to Scan Times Square Area for Crime." *The New York Times.* June 20.

Schwartzman, Paul. 1998. "11 More Cameras Sprout in Washington Sq. Park." *The New York Times.* April 24.

Simon, Jonathan. 1987. "The Emergence of a Risk Society: Insurance, Law and the State." *Socialist Review.* 95: 61-89.

Skenazy, Lauren. 2004. "New Reality TV from the MTA?" *The Daily News*. March 31.

Smith, Gavin John Douglas. 2008. "Empowered Watchers or Disempowered Workers?: The Ambiguities of Power within Technologies of Security" In *Technologies of Insecurity: The Surveillance of Everyday Life,* edited by Katja Franko Aas, Helene Oppen Gundhus and Heidi Mork Lomell, 125-146. New York: Routledge-Cavendish.

Smith, Jeff H. 1994. *Managing Privacy: Information Technology and Corporate America.* Chapel Hill: The University of North Carolina Press.

Smith, Mary. 1996. *Crime Prevention through Environmental Design in Parking Facilities.* National Institute of Justice (NCJ157 310). Washington, D.C.

Smith, Neil. 1996. *The New Urban Frontier: Gentrification and the Revanchist City.* New York: Routledge.

Smith, Victoria. 2002. "West Virginia District Links School Cameras to Emergency Responders." *Associated Press State and Local Wire*. October 8.

Solove, Daniel. 2004. *The Digital Person: Technology and Privacy in the Information Age*. New York: New York University Press.

Solove, Daniel. 2008. *Understanding Privacy.* Cambridge, MA: Harvard University Press.

Spielman, Fred. 2004. "Cameras on Street Sweepers Considered for Nailing Scofflaws." *Chicago Sun-Times*. September 14.

Spielvogel, John. 2002. "Cameras on Campuses Bring School Safety into Sharp Focus." *The San Diego Union Tribune.* September 15.

Staples, William. 2000. *Everyday Surveillance: Vigilance and Visibility in Postmodern Life.* Lanham, MD: Rowman and Littlefield Publishers.

Surette, Ray. 1998. *Media, Crime and Criminal Justice: Images and Realities.* Belmont, CA: Wadsworth.

Tagg, John. 1993. *The Burden of Representation: Essays and Photographies and Histories.* Minneapolis: University of Minnesota Press.

Taylor, Ralph and Adele Harrell. 1995. *Physical Environment and Crime. National Institute of Justice (NCJ 157 311).* Washington, D.C.

"Under close watch." 2007. *Government Security.* August 1.

United States Department of Interior, National Park Service, United States Park Police. 2002. *United States Park Police Closed Circuit Television Policy.* Washington, DC.

van der Ploeg, Irma. 2006. "Borderline Identities: The Enrollment of Bodies in the Technological Reconstruction of Borders." In *Surveillance and Security: Technological Politics and Power in Everyday Life*, edited by Torin Monahan, 177-194. New York: Routledge.

van Gelder, Lawrence. 1994. "School Safety Division Tries to Hold the Line." *The New York Times.* September 15.

van Sickler, Mary. 1999. "Video Surveillance Grows as Technology Cheapens." *The Ledger.* January 17.

Vlahos, James. 2008. "Surveillance Society: New High Tech Cameras are Watching You." *Popular Mechanics*. http://www .popularmechanics.com/technology/military _law/4236865.html.

Ward, Janet. 1998. "Beyond the Big brother Syndrome." *American City and County:* CCTV Supplement. October 1. http://www .americancityandcounty.com/mag/government_beyond_big _brother/

Warner, Marien Mary. 1997. *Photography and its Critics: A Cultural History, 1839-1900*. Cambridge University Press.

Warren, Samuel D. and Louis D. Brandeis. 1890. "The Right to Privacy." *Harvard Law Review*. 4 (5): 193-220.

Washington Post/ABC News. 2007. "Washington Post ABC News Poll." http://media.washingtonpost.com/wp-srv/politics/ssi/polls /postpoll_072307.html

Webb. Maureen. 2007. *Illusions of Security: Global Surveillance and Democracy in the Post-9/11 World.* City Lights Publishers.

Weintraub, Jeff Alan. 1997. "The Theory and Politics of the Public/Private Distinction." In *Public and Private in Thought and*

Practice: Perspectives on a Grand Dichotomy, edited by Jeff Alan Weintraub and Krishan Kumar, 1-42. Chicago: University of Chicago Press.

Westin, Alan. 1967. *Privacy and Freedom*. New York: Atheneum.

Whitaker, Reg. 1999. *The End of Privacy: How Total Surveillance is Becoming a Reality*. New York: The New Press.

Whitaker, Reg. 2006. "A Faustian Bargain? America and the Dream of Total Information Awareness." In *The New Politics of Surveillance and Visibility*, edited by Kevin D. Haggerty and Richard V. Ericson. 141-170. Toronto: University of Toronto Press.

Winston, Ali. 2007. "Students on Camera, Schools under Watch." *City Limits*. April 9. http://www. citylimits.org /content /articles /viewarticle.cfm? article_id=3304.

Winston, Ali. 2008. "What do Cameras Cure? System Gets Own Scrutiny." *City Limits*. January 21. http://citylimits.org /content /articles/ viewarticle.cfm?article_id=3483.

Yesil, Bilge. 2006. "Watching Ourselves: Video Surveillance, Urban Space, and Self-Responsibilization." *Cultural Studies*, 20 (4-5): 400-416.

Zogby International. 2002. "Zogby's Tracking Report Americans maintain opposition to phone tapping, continue approval for random car searches." March 6. http://www.zogby.com /search/ReadNews.cfm?ID=541

Zogby International. 2006. "Americans Ponder Tighter Security Measures." September 9. http://www.angus-reid.com/polls/view /13072/americans_ponder_tighter_security_measures.

Zureik, Elia and Mark Salter. 2005. *Global Surveillance and Policing: Borders, Security, Identity*. Devon, UK: Willan Publishing.

Index

CPSIA information can be obtained at www.ICGtesting.com
Printed in the USA
BVOW071231041112

304221BV00002B/6/P

9 781593 323707